Reflections upon Religion

Reflections upon Religion

Seungbae Park, Ph.D.

Philosophy Professor
Ulsan National Institute of Science and Technology
The Republic of Korea

PREFACE

This book is intended to be a useful philosophy of religion textbook for undergraduate students who major in science and engineering.

Unlike other philosophy of religion books, this book often combines traditional topics in philosophy of religion with scientific theories, such as evolutionary theory and the Big Bang theory. For this reason, science and engineering majors will be more excited to discuss traditional topics in philosophy of religion.

I do not expect that the readers of this book will be philosophy majors. As a consequence, philosophical jargons are kept to a minimum. In case I inevitably use one, I define it and offer examples to illustrate it.

As a result of reading this book, students will increase their ability to think critically and creatively about God and religion. Demonstration is the best way to help them increase such an ability. In this spirit, I criticize distinguished thinkers' views about God and religion, and defend alternatives to them.

I sometimes develop new topics about God and religion so that readers can be engaged in new debates about them. Such debates will cast new light on them.

There are study questions at the end of each chapter. They are intended to stimulate readers to think for themselves about God and religion and to go beyond what I said in the book.

I thank the University of Maryland and UNIST for the chance to teach philosophy of religion courses. I could not write this book without my teaching experiences at those universities. Finally, I thank Professor John Park in Department of Philosophy at California State University – Sacramento for useful comments on an earlier draft of this book.

Ulsan

The Republic of Korea Seungbae Park

CONTENTS

Chapter (1-15)

Chapter (16-30)

CHAPTER 1

Basic Terms

1. Belief

We have many beliefs. We believe that the sky is blue, that the earth is round, and that God exists. A belief is one of many mental states: pain, hunger, thirst, hope, love, etc. A belief possesses a distinctive feature, a characteristic that sets it apart from other mental states, viz., it can be true or false. It is a true belief, for example, that Moscow is located in Russia. It is a false belief that Moscow is located in the U.S. Contrast a belief with a hunger. A hunger is not a kind of mental state that can be true or false. It is meaningless to say that a hunger is true or false.

2. True vs. Useful

Under what condition is a belief true? What feature do true beliefs have in common? In this section, I introduce Aristotle's answers to these questions.

According to Aristotle, a belief is true if and only if it corresponds to reality, i.e., a belief is true when it matches up with the world. Consider the following examples:

True Beliefs

- The earth is round.
- Water is H_2O.
- Plato was Aristotle's teacher.

These beliefs are true because they correspond to the world. The world is the truth-maker for them, i.e., the world makes them true. To say so means that if the world were different, they would be false. For example, if the earth were flat, it would be false that the earth is round. Contrast the true beliefs with the following false beliefs:

False Beliefs

- The earth is flat.
- Water is H_3O.
- Aristotle was Plato's teacher.

These beliefs are false because they do not correspond to the world. The world makes them false. To say so means that if the world were different, they might be true. For example, if the earth were flat, it would be true that the earth is flat. In sum, true beliefs correspond to the world, whereas false beliefs do not. This theory of truth is called "the correspondence theory of truth." It was propounded by Aristotle.

A true belief seems to be useful, and a false belief seems to be useless. Suppose that your train is scheduled to leave at 12:00. You believe that it is scheduled to leave at 12:00. As a result, you show up in the train station on time and catch your train. Your true belief is useful. Suppose, in contrast, that your train is scheduled to leave at 12:00. You believe that your train is scheduled to leave at

14:00. As a result, you miss your train. Your false belief is useless.

A true belief, however, is not always useful, and a false belief is not always useless. In certain cases, a true belief is useless, and a false belief is useful. Imagine that you catch the train thanks to the true belief that your train was scheduled to leave at 12:00. However, the train is derailed due to an earthquake, and all the passengers, including you, die. In such a case, the true belief is useless. Imagine, by contrast, that you miss the train due to the false belief that your train is scheduled to leave at 14:00. As a result, you do not die. In such a case, the false belief is useful.

Suppose that you believe that God exists. Is your belief true or false? Is it useful or useless? This book attempts to answer these questions. Different thinkers would have different answers to these questions. Some may think that belief in God is true and useful. Some may think that it is false but useful. Some may think that it is false and useless.

In any event, it is wrong to say that it is useful to believe God exists, and thus it is true that he exists. Although it is useful to believe that he exists, it might be false that he exists. Usefulness and truth should be kept apart from each other.

3. Knowledge

Knowledge is power, as Francis Bacon (1561-1626) famously claimed. Science pursues knowledge. Scientists are those who aim to *know* about the world. But what is knowledge? Under what condition can we say that we know something? How does knowledge differ from belief? I introduce Plato's answers to these questions in this section.

Truth is a component of knowledge, and thus where there is no truth, there is no knowledge. Consider the following list of false statements:

The List of False Statements

- The earth is flat.
- Water is H_3O.
- Aristotle was Plato's teacher.

It does not make sense to say that we know that the earth is flat, that water is H_3O, and that Aristotle was Plato's teacher, while it makes sense to say that we know that the earth is round, that water is H_2O, and that Plato was Aristotle's teacher. These examples indicate that truth is a component of knowledge.

Justification is another component of knowledge, i.e., thus where there is no justification, there is no knowledge. Suppose that there is life on Mars, and that you have no evidence for the belief that there is life on Mars, but that somehow you believe that there is life on Mars. In such a case, you can say, "I believe there is life on Mars," but not "I know there is life on Mars." You can say "I know that there is life on Mars," only when you have sufficient evidence for the belief that there is life on Mars. As another example, suppose that you are a police officer. You believe that Ted Bundy committed murder, but you do not have evidence for your belief. In such a case, you can say, "I believe Ted Bundy committed murder," but not "I know Ted Bundy committed murder." Suppose, however, that you have sufficient evidence for the belief that Ted Bundy committed murder. For example, you witnessed Ted Bundy commit murder, and you have a knife on which there is Ted Bundy's fingerprint. In such a case, you can say, "I know Ted Bundy committed murder." These examples indicate that justification is a component of knowledge.

Belief is another component of knowledge, and thus where there is no belief, there is no knowledge. It is a contradiction to say, "I know Ted Bundy committed murder, but I don't believe Ted Bundy committed murder." To take another example, it is a contradiction to say, "I know some swans are black, but I don't believe some swans are black." These examples indicate that belief is a component of knowledge.

To sum up, truth, justification, and belief are the components of knowledge, i.e., knowledge is composed of truth, justification, and belief. For this reason, Plato defines knowledge as a justified true belief. On his account, you *know* that p, when it is *true* that p, when you have *good evidence* for p, and that you *believe* that p, where p is a proposition, that which can be true or false. For example, you know that Seoul is located in South Korea, when it is true that Seoul is located in South Korea, when you have good evidence that Seoul is located in South Korea, and when you believe that Seoul is located in South Korea. If one or more of these three components is missing, you do not know that Seoul is located in South Korea.

Belief is a component of knowledge. So the requirement for knowing that p is higher than the requirement for believing that p. You can say, for example, "I believe the earth is round," even if you do not have evidence for the proposition that the earth is round, and even if the proposition is false. In contrast, you cannot say, "I know that the earth is round," if you do not have sufficient evidence for the proposition that the earth is round, and if the proposition is false. In other words, to say, "I know the earth is round," requires that you should have good evidence for the proposition, and that the proposition should be true.

Let me apply Plato's analysis of knowledge to a religious example. You can say, "I believe God exists," even if you do not have evidence for the proposition that he exists, and even if the proposition is false. In contrast, you cannot say, "I know God exists," if you do not have sufficient evidence for the proposition, and if the proposition is false. In other words, to say, "I know God exists," requires that you should have good evidence for the proposition, and that the proposition should be true.

There is an important difference among knowledge, a justified belief, and a belief. To say that I *know* that it will rain tomorrow implies that it is 100% probable that it will rain. To say that I am *justified* in believing that it will rain tomorrow implies that it is likely that it will rain tomorrow. To say that I *believe* that it will rain tomorrow implies that no probability is assigned to the statement that it will rain tomorrow.

Can we say, "I know God exists"? Or can we say, "I am justified in believing God exists"? Or can we only say, "I believe God exists"? To put it otherwise, do we have the knowledge that he exists? Or do we have a justified belief that he exists? Or do we have merely the belief that he exists? This book attempts to answer this question.

4. Argument

Suppose that you believe that the earth is round, and that your evidence for the belief is that the earth's shadow cast on the moon is round. The evidence and the belief can be reconstructed as the following set of statements:

The earth's shadow cast on the moon is round.
∴ The earth is round.

This set of statements is an argument. An argument is a set of statements some of which are premises and one of which is the conclusion. A premise is the evidence for the conclusion, i.e., it is the reason for believing that the conclusion is true. In an argument, there is only one conclusion, but there can be more than one premise.

An argument can be strong or weak depending on whether premises justify the conclusion. They justify it if and only if they are true, and it follows from them. Therefore, an argument is strong if and only if its premises are true and its conclusions follow from them. By contrast, it is weak if and only if one of its premises is false or its conclusion does not follow from its premises.

Do we have a strong argument or only a weak argument for belief in God? This book attempts to answer this question.

5. Theism, Atheism, and Skepticism

There are three attitudes that you can take toward God. They are fleshed out one by one in this section.

(i) You can believe that he exists, in which case you are a believer or a theist. To state it differently, you can hold the view called "theism" according to which he exists. Theists have the burden of showing that he exists, i.e., they have the burden of constructing a strong argument for his existence. They cannot ask their opponents to prove that he does not exist. To use an analogy, if scientists believe that there is a life on Mars, they have the burden of showing that there is a life on Mars. They should not ask their opponents to prove that there is no life on Mars.

(ii) You can disbelieve that God exists, i.e., you can believe that he does not exist, in which case you are an atheist. To put it differently, you can hold the view called "atheism" according to which he does not exist. Atheists have the burden of showing that he does not exist, i.e., they have the burden of constructing a strong argument for his nonexistence. They cannot ask their opponents to prove that he exists. To use an analogy, if scientists believe that there is no life on Mars, they have the burden of showing that there is no life on Mars. They should not ask their opponents to prove that there is life on Mars.

(iii) You can be skeptical or agnostic that God exists, in which case you are a skeptic or an agnostic. To put it another way, you can hold the view called "skepticism" or "agnosticism" according to which we do not know whether he exists or not, i.e., we do not have a strong argument for his existence and his nonexistence. Skeptics have the burden of showing that theists' arguments and atheists' arguments are weak. To use an analogy, if you are skeptical about whether there is a life on Mars, you have the burden of refuting the arguments that some have provided to show that there is a life on Mars, and the arguments that others have provided to show that there is no life on Mars.

It is a perennial topic in philosophy of religion which of the three positions – theism, atheism, and skepticism – is more reasonable than others. Readers will be exposed to several arguments for and against the existence of God in this book.

6. Summary

A belief is a peculiar mental statement in that it can be true or false. On Aristotle's account, a true belief corresponds to the world while a false belief does not. A belief can also be useful or useless. A true belief might be useless, and a false belief might be useful. On Plato's account, knowledge is a justified true belief. An argument, which is composed of premises and the conclusion, can be strong or weak. Theists believe that we have a strong argument for the belief that God exists. Atheists believe that we have a strong argument for the belief that he does not exist. Skeptics believe that we have no such arguments.

Study Questions

1. What is the distinctive feature of a belief? Give your own examples of true, false, useful, and useless beliefs. Give your own example of an argument.

2. What are the three components of knowledge? How do belief and knowledge differ from each other? Provide your own examples. Can we say, "I know God exists"? Can we say, "I am justified in believing that God exists?" Or can we only say, "I believe God exists"? What are the three attitudes we can take toward God?

CHAPTER 2

The Attributes of God

1. Prelude

There are many religions in the world, and different religions worship different deities. For example, Christianity, Islam, and Hinduism worship God, Allah, and Vishnu, respectively. By "God," I mean the deity that Christianity worships throughout this book. By "God," I do not mean other deities, such as Allah and Vishnu.

Christianity attributes three important properties to God. They are omnipotence, omniscience, and omnibenevolence. In plain English, Christianity asserts that he can do anything, knows everything, and is perfectly good. In addition to these three properties, he allegedly has other properties, as will become clear in this chapter. This chapter discusses the philosophical issues that arise from his putative properties.

2. Omnipotent, Omniscient, and Omnibenevolent

Atheists have raised a few objections to the view that God is omnipotent. Can he commit suicide? Can he create another God? Can he create a stone that is so heavy that he cannot lift it up? Carlo Alvaro (2021, p. 10) replies that God cannot do those things, and yet he is omnipotent. On his account, even an omnipotent being cannot certain things. For example, he cannot create a married bachelor, given that a bachelor is, by definition, unmarried. Just as God is omnipotent even if he cannot create a married bachelor, so he is omnipotent even if he cannot commit suicide, cannot create another God, and cannot create the stone.

How about the view that God is omnibenevolent? This view on him seems to be incompatible with what the Bible says. On the one hand, the Bible tells us to love our neighbors and to pray to those who persecute us. On the other hand, it tells slaves to be obedient to their masters. It says, for example, "Servants, submit yourselves to your masters with all respect" (1 Peter 2:18). It also states that if a bride is not a virgin on the wedding night, "the men of her town shall stone her to death" (Deuteronomy 22:21). An omnibenevolent being would not support slavery and would not encourage men to kill non-virgin brides. It appears that God is not omnibenevolent.

Let me turn to the view that God is omniscient. If he is omniscient, it is difficult to "conceive of a satisfactory justification for petitionary prayer" (Stump, 1979, p. 81). A petitionary prayer is a prayer in which a prayer (a person who prays) asks him to do something for her. It is a petitionary prayer, for example, that you ask him to help you to pass a job interview. To say that God is omniscient implies that he knows everything that will happen in the future, which in turn implies that he knows whether you will pass or fail the job interview. As noted in Chapter 1, knowledge is justified *true* belief. It follows that if God knows that you will pass the job interview, it is 100% probable that you will pass the job interview. If he knows that you will fail the job interview, it is 100% probable that you will fail the job interview. The following dilemma can be construct against your petitionary prayer.

Either God knows that you will pass the job interview, or he knows that you will fail the job interview. On the one hand, if he knows that you will pass the job interview, it is 100% probable that you will pass the job interview. You will pass the job interview, even if you do not pray to him that you will pass the job interview. Your prayer does not make any difference to the outcome of the job interview, and it is only a waste of time to pray to him. On the other hand, if he knows that you will fail the job interview, it is 100% probable that you will fail the job interview. You will fail the job interview, even if you pray to him that you will pass the job interview. Your prayer does not make any difference to the outcome of the job interview, and it is only a waste of time to pray to him. Therefore, it does not matter whether he knows that you will pass or fail the job interview. Your prayer does not make any difference to the outcome of the job interview, and it is only a waste of time to pray to him. In short, your petitionary prayer is pointless.

Suppose that you pray to God that you will pass the job interview, and that you pass the job interview. You may think that you were scheduled to fail the job interview, but that he changed the outcome of the job interview due to your prayer. In reality, however, he did not change the outcome of the job interview. He knew all along that you would pass the job interview. It was 100% probable that you would pass the job interview. Accordingly, your prayer did not make any contribution to the outcome of the job interview, and it was only a waste of time for you to pray to him.

Suppose that you pray to God that you will pass the job interview, but that you fail the job interview. You may think that you should have prayed harder to him. To state it differently, you may think that you were scheduled to pass the job interview, but he changed the outcome of the job interview because you did not pray to him harder. In reality, however, he did not change the outcome of the job interview. He knew all along that you would fail the job interview. It was 100% probable that you would fail the job interview. Consequently, your harder prayer could not have made any difference to the outcome of the job interview, and it would have been only a waste of time for you to have prayed harder to God.

Theists might argue that God is omnipotent, and thus that he can replace a future event with another future event. For example, he can replace your failing the job interview with your passing the job interview. It follows that your petitionary prayer increases the probability that you will pass the job interview.

Atheists would object that God is omniscient, and thus that he knows whether he will replace a future event with another future event. For example, he knows whether he will replace your failing the job interview with your passing the job interview. If he knows that he will, it is 100% probable that you will pass the job interview. If he knows that he will not, it is 100% probable that you will fail the job interview. Either way, your petitionary prayer neither increases the probability that you will pass the job interview nor decreases the probability that you will fail the job interview.

3. Other Properties

Some theists claim that God is a transcendental being, i.e., that he transcends human understanding. We cannot understand him any more than ants can understand humans. He is an infinite being, whereas humans are finite beings. The finite beings' minds are not powerful enough to understand the infinite being. Accordingly, it is natural that we cannot understand why he supports slavery and the murder of non-virgin brides. It is a manifestation of human arrogance for atheists to say that humans can understand him.

This view on God is vulnerable to the following objection. How can theists know that he is a transcendental being? They are finite beings just like atheists. Consequently, they cannot know that he is a transcendental being any more than atheists can know that he is a transcendental being. Theists' minds are not powerful enough to understand the infinite being. It is a manifestation of human arrogance for theists to say that we cannot understand him. It appears that if he is a transcendental being, both theists and atheists should only be silent about him, i.e., they should say nothing about him. This conclusion has the implication that we should neither say that he exists nor that he does not.

Another objection can be raised to the view that God is a transcendental being. The Bible makes many claims about him. For example, it says that he created the world:

> In the beginning, God created the heavens and the earth. The earth was without form and void, and darkness was over the face of the deep. And the Spirit of God was hovering over the face of the waters. And God said, 'Let there be light,' and there was light. (Genesis 1:1-3)

Those who claim that he is a transcendental being owe us an account of what we are to make of such verses in the Bible. It is arbitrary to say that he is a transcendental being, but that we can trust what the Bible says about him.

Let me turn to the view that God is a *necessary* being as opposed to a *contingent* being. A necessary being is a being that must exist, while a contingent being is a being that happens to exist and might not exist. Ordinary objects, such as trees and computers, are contingent beings, given that it is possible that they might not exist. Unlike ordinary objects, God is a necessary being, i.e., he must exist, and it is false that he happens to exist, and that he might not exist.

A few interesting consequences follow from the view that God is a necessary being. First, he cannot commit suicide. If he commits suicide, he will cease to exist. However, it is impossible for him not to exist, and thus he cannot commit suicide. Second, he does not have a creator, i.e., no one created him. After all, to say that he has a creator implies that he did not exist before he was created. However, it was impossible for him not to exist, and thus he does not have a creator. Third, he is eternal. He existed for an infinitely long time, and he will exist for an infinitely long time.

Atheists would rejoin that if he is a necessary being, the universe is also a necessary being. On their account, it is not possible for the universe not to exist any more than it is possible for him not to exist. Theists would object that we can imagine that the universe does not exist, and thus that the universe is a contingent being. Atheists would reply that we can also imagine that he does not exist, and thus that he, if existent, is also a contingent being. In short, he and the universe are in the same boat.

Finally, God purportedly created the world, i.e., he is allegedly the creator of the world. The world would not exist, had it not been for him. Thus, the world owes its existence to him. He created not only the world but also human beings. Human beings would not exist, had it not been for him. Thus, they owe their existence to him.

This view on God invites the following two objections. First, who created God? If he does not have a creator, the universe does not have a creator, either. If he is eternal, the universe is also eternal. Second, Ockham's razor favors the view that the universe exists while God does not over the view that both the universe and God exist. Ockham's razor is the principle that we should choose a simple hypothesis over a complex one.

4. Summary

God is omnipotent even if he cannot do absurd things, such as committing suicide and creating another God. Some verses in the Bible does not go hand in hand with the view that he is omnibenevolent. If he is omniscient, a petitionary prayer is pointless. In other words, there is a conflict between the belief that he is omniscient and the belief that a petitionary prayer makes a difference to a future event. If he is a transcendental being, even theists should be reticent about him. He and the universe are in the same boat vis-à-vis the issue of whether they are necessary beings, and the issue of whether they have creators.

Study Questions

1. Raise objections to the view that God is omnipotent, omniscient, and omnibenevolent. If you were theists, how would you reply to them?

2. Raise objections to the view that God is a transcendental being, a necessary being, and the creator of the world. If you were theists, how would you reply to them?

References

Alvaro, C. (2021). Atheism as an extreme rejection of rational evidence for the existence of God. *The Heythrop Journal*, 62(2), 1-16.

Stump, E. (1979). Petitionary prayer. *American Philosophical Quarterly*, 16(2), 81-91.

CHAPTER 3

Design, Miracles, and Religious Experiences

1. Overview

Philosophers constructed several arguments for the existence of God in the history of philosophy. This chapter unpacks and examines three of them. They are the argument from design, the argument from miracles, and the argument from religious experiences.

2. The Argument from Design

We have eyebrows on our forehead. Why do they exist? Theists might suggest that the eyebrows exist so that they can protect the eyes from the raindrops and the drops of perspiration, i.e., that the eyebrows exist to serve the purpose of protecting the eyes from the raindrops and the drops of perspiration. We should be thankful to God for creating the eyebrows. In this example of eyebrows, we can see the spirit of the argument from design.

The argument from design was constructed, without being endorsed, by David Hume (1779/1998, p. 15). It starts from the two observational facts. First, an organism is complex. Its different parts are intricately connected with one another, and they work together to sustain the organism. Second, an ecosystem is harmonious. The different organisms in the ecosystem are intricately connected with one another, and they work together to sustain the ecosystem. There can be two rival hypotheses explaining these observational facts. The first one is the design hypothesis according to which an intelligent designer, God, created complex organisms and the harmonious ecosystem. The second one is the random hypothesis according to which random physical processes turned the lumps of matter into complex organisms and the harmonious ecosystem, i.e., it was an accident that the lumps of matter became complex organisms and the harmonious ecosystem.

Which hypothesis is more plausible, the design hypothesis or the random hypothesis? William Paley (1802, pp. 1-2) appeals to the following analogy to argue that the design hypothesis is more plausible than the random hypothesis. Suppose that you came across a stone in a heath. A stone is a simple thing, so you would not infer that it was created by an intelligent designer. Suppose, by contrast, that you found a watch in a heath. It is a complex thing. Its parts are intricately connected with one another so that it is well-suited to the task of keeping the time. If you opened it up and examined its inner working, you would infer that it was created by an intelligent designer. You would not infer that random physical processes produced the watch, a complex thing. Just as you would infer that the watch was created by an intelligent designer, so you should infer that complex organisms and the harmonious ecosystem were created by an intelligent designer. The intelligent designer who created the watch is a human being, whereas the intelligent designer who created complex organisms and the harmonious ecosystem is God.

Darwin's response to the argument from design is to offer a

third hypothesis according to which natural selection, not God, produced complex organisms and the harmonious ecosystem. Natural selection occurs when there is "heritable variation in fitness" (Sober, 2018, p. 9). Variation is a random process, i.e., it occurs without regard to the need of organisms. By contrast, natural selection is not a random process. It does not select any organisms, and it rather selects only certain organisms, viz., the fittest ones. In other words, natural selection produces only adapted organisms. This hypothesis is different from the random hypothesis as well as from the design hypothesis.

Which is better, the design hypothesis or Darwin's hypothesis? There are biological phenomena that Darwin's hypothesis can explain but the design hypothesis cannot (Sober, 2018, pp. 39–40). For example, gill slits appear on human embryos and then disappear. This phenomenon is explicable on Darwin's hypothesis according to which humans' distant ancestors were fish, whereas it is inexplicable on the design hypothesis according to which our ancestors were designed by God and their morphologies did not change.

3. The Argument from Miracles

Let me turn to the argument from miracles. It asserts that miracles occur, that only God can make miracles, and thus that he exists. What would be examples of miracles? A woman cannot lift up a car, but a mother can lift up a car to rescue her child. Such an event might be called "a miracle." Our ancestors observed a solar eclipse. They could not explain why the sun disappeared. They thought that a solar eclipse was a miracle (Vainstub et al., 2020). Strictly speaking, however, such events do not count as miracles.

Hume (1779/1998, p. 111) suggests that a miracle is an event that violates a law of nature, and that we can never be certain that a law of nature is violated. Suppose that an event occurs, and that it cannot be explained by *known* laws of nature. Does it follow that it is a miracle? The answer is "No," given that there might be *unknown* laws of nature which can explain the putative miracle. For example, some primitive people, uninformed of modern astronomy, observe a meteorite falling from the sky. They believe that it is a miracle that a stone falls down from the sky. Such an example shows that even if science cannot explain a puzzling event now, it might explain it in the future. Therefore, we can never be sure that a miracle has occurred.

How would theists reply to Hume's foregoing objection to the argument from miracles? They would appeal to the Bible to argue that miracles, as defined by Hume, occurred. According to the Bible, Jesus Christ did many things that violated the laws of nature. For example, he turned water into wine (John 2:1-11). He brought the dead back to life (Luke 7:11-18, Matthew 9:18-26). He stopped the storm (Matthew 8:23-27). He walked on water (Matthew 14:25-27). Such events clearly violate laws of nature. Therefore, we can be confident that miracles occur.

This reply raises an interesting issue of whether we can trust everything that the Bible says. Some verses in the Bible are agreeable. For example, it says that "You shall love your neighbor as yourself" (Mark, 12:21). Other verses in the Bible are disagreeable. For example, God commands genocide against Amalekites for waylaying Israelites, saying "Do not spare them; put to death men and women, children and infants, cattle and sheep, camels and donkeys" (Samuel 15:3). There are controversial verses in the Bible. For example, it says that "God created the heavens and the earth" (Genesis 1:1). Some people agree, while other people disagree, to this view on the origin of the universe, as will become clear in Chapter 6. Therefore, we cannot completely trust what the Bible says, and it is doubtful whether Jesus Christ really did what the Bible says that he did.

Moreover, different religions have different scriptures. The scripture for Christianity is the Bible, the scripture for Islam is the Quran, and the scripture for Hinduism is the Vedas. Should we trust all of them? Or should we select one of them? If we should choose, which one should we? Why? Theists might answer that we may choose the one that our parents or friends have chosen. A problem with this answer is that our parents or friends did not have good evidence for having chosen one scripture over the others, i.e., that they were in no better epistemic situation than we are with respect to the issue of which scripture should be chosen over the others.

4. The Argument from Religious Experiences

The argument from religious experiences holds that we can perceive God, so he exists. Some deeply religious people claim that they had religious experiences. St. John, for example, describes his religious experience as follows:

> The end I have in view is the divine Embracing, the union of the soul with the divine Substance. In this loving, obscure knowledge God unites Himself with the soul eminently and divinely. This knowledge consists in a certain contact of the soul with the Divinity, and it is God Himself Who is then felt and tasted, though not manifestly and distinctly, as it will in glory. But this touch of knowledge and of sweetness is so deep and so profound that it penetrates into the inmost substance of the soul. (Kurtz, 1991, p. 96)

In this excerpt, St. John opines that he has seen God, that his soul became one with him, that the experience was sweet, and that the experience had a deep impact on his soul.

What are we to make of those who claim that they experienced God? We can admit that they had a certain experience, but we can doubt that they had the experience of him. This skepticism is grounded in the following considerations. First, there are many religions in the world. Christians, Muslims, and Hinduists claim that they had the experiences of God, Allah, and Vishnu, respectively. It is not clear who we should trust (Schick and

Vaughn, 2010, p. 495).

Second, there is an important difference between a religious experience and a scientific experience. A scientific experience is reproducible, whereas a religious experience is not. Suppose that scientists perform an experiment, and that they obtain the experimental result. They publish a paper in which they describe the experimental procedure which led to the experimental result. Other scientists, who read the paper, can follow the experimental procedure, and can produce the same experimental result. In this sense, a scientific experience is reproducible. The same thing cannot be done about a religious experience.

Theists would retort that only those who went through a religious training can have a religious experience, and that the religious training involves a lot of time and energy. To use an analogy, English professors spend a lot of time and energy to acquire the ability to appreciate English poems. As a result, they can have a sweet feeling when they read English poems. By contrast, children who could not go through the literary training cannot have a sweet feeling when they read English poems. Similarly, those who did not go through a long and arduous religious training cannot have a religious experience. You should keep training yourself until you have a religious experience.

5. Summary

The argument from design holds that just as a watch-maker designed a watch, so God designed human beings. However, evolutionary theory holds that complex organisms have evolved from simple organisms. The argument from miracles holds that since miracles occur, God exists. However, we cannot know that an event has violated a law of nature. The Bible reports some putative miracles. However, there are some disagreeable verses in the Bible. The argument from religious experiences holds that we can see God, and thus he exists. However, believers of different religions claim that they have experience their own deities. Moreover, religious experiences differ from scientific experiences in that religious experiences are not reproducible while scientific experiences are reproducible. Theists would say that if we go through the right religious training, we can experience God.

Study Questions

1. State the argument from design. Is it convincing to you? Why? Why not?

2. Explicate the arguments from miracles and religious experiences. Do you accept or reject them? Why?

References

Hume, D. (1779/1998). *Dialogues concerning natural religion*. Indianapolis: Hackett.

Kurtz, P. (1991). *The transcendental temptation*. Buffalo, NY: Prometheus Books.

Paley, W. (1802). *Natural theology: Or, evidences of the existence and attributes of the deity*. London: Gregg International Publishers Limited.

Schick, T. Jr. and Vaughn, L. (2010). *Doing philosophy: An introduction through thought experiments*. New York, NY: The McGraw-Hill Companies.

Sober, E. (2018). *Philosophy of biology*. New York, NY: Routledge.

Vainstub, D., Yizhaq, H., & Avner, U. (2020). The miracle of the sun and moon in Joshua 10 as a solar eclipse. *Vetus Testamentum*, 70(4-5), 722-751.

CHAPTER

4

The Ontological Argument

1. Overview

In this chapter, we go over two versions of the ontological argument for the existence of God. One is advanced by a medieval philosopher, St. Anselm (1033–1109), and the other is advanced by a contemporary philosopher, Alvin Plantinga (1932–present). Both versions are problematic, as with other arguments for the existence of God.

2. St. Anselm's Version

St. Anselm's (1958, p. 8) variant of the ontological argument goes as follows. God is the greatest of all the things that we can conceive of. We can conceive of God existing in the world and God existing in our minds. God existing in the world is greater than God existing in our minds. God is, by definition, the greatest being. Therefore, God exists in the world. To put it differently, God existing in the world is perfect while God existing in our minds is imperfect. God is, by definition, the perfect being. Therefore, God exists in the world.

Gaunilo (1968), St. Anselm's contemporary monk, argues that the ontological argument for the existence of God is similar to the following absurd argument for the existence of the perfect island. The perfect island existing in the world is greater than the perfect island existing in our minds. After all, you can spend your vacation in the perfect island existing in the world, but not in the perfect island existing in our minds. Therefore, the perfect island exists in the world. However, this conclusion is false, i.e., the perfect island does not exist. Just as this argument for the existence of the perfect island is fallacious, so the ontological argument for the existence of God is fallacious.

St. Anselm rejoins that there is an important difference between God and the perfect island. He is the greatest of all the things, including the perfect island, i.e., nothing is greater than him. By contrast, there are some things greater than the perfect island. For example, he and angels are greater than the perfect island. This difference between him and the perfect island entitles us to say that he must exist in the world in order to be perfect, but that the perfect island need not exist in the world in order to be perfect.

3. Plantinga's Version

Alvin Plantinga (1974) has constructed a new version of the ontological argument. According to him, God is, by definition, the greatest being, i.e., he "possesses a maximal degree of greatness" (Plantinga, 1974, p. 203). Imagine that there are two Gods. One is a contingent being, i.e., it is possible for him not to exist, which implies that he can commit suicide. The other is a necessary being, i.e., it is impossible for him not to exist, which implies that he cannot commit suicide. Which one is greater? Obviously, the necessary one is greater than the contingent one. Given that God is the greatest being, he is the necessary being, i.e., he necessarily exists. So Plantinga says.

4. A Critique of Both Versions

What are we to make of St. Anselm's old version and Plantinga's new version of the ontological argument? In my view, critics can object that both St. Anselm and Plantinga have the burden of explaining why God is elusive. If he is the greatest being, he should appear to us and interact with us, but he does not. It is mysterious why he does not show himself to us. Suppose that there are two Gods. One is visible to us, while the other is invisible to us, and other things are equal. Obviously, the first one is greater than the second one. Given that God is the greatest being, he should be visible to us.

If you are not yet convinced of my foregoing objection to the ontological argument, consider the following analogy. Suppose that there are two presidential candidates in the next election of your country. One is visible, while the other is invisible, and other conditions are equal. Which candidate is greater? Who would you vote for? The answer to these questions is obvious. The visible candidate is greater than the invisible one. By parity of reasoning, visible God is greater than invisible God.

On St. Anselm's variant of the ontological argument, existence makes something greater. On Plantinga's variant of the ontological argument, necessary existence makes something greater. In my view, if St. Anselm and Plantinga are right, visibility also makes something greater. It is *ad hoc* to say that existence and necessary existence make something greater, but that visibility does not. To state it otherwise, justification is required for the position that existence and necessary existence make something greater, but that visibility does not.

5. Summary

According to St. Anselm, God existing in the world is greater than God existing in our minds. God is, by definition, the greatest being. Therefore, he exists. Gaunilo objects that the perfect island existing in the world is greater than the perfect island existing in our minds. However, the perfect island does not exist. The same holds for God. According to Plantinga, necessary God is greater than contingent God. God is, by definition, the greatest being. Therefore, he necessarily exists. Regarding both versions, I objected that if he is the greatest being, he should be visible to us. However, he is not visible to us. Therefore, he does not exist.

Study Questions

1. Summarize and respond to the debate between St. Anselm and Gaunilo. Who is right? Why? Suppose that someone claims that he has the greatest girlfriend, but that she is invisible. How would you

respond to him?

2. Plantinga argues that God is the greatest being, and thus that he necessarily exists. How do you respond to his argument? Suppose that someone claims that she has the greatest parents, but that they are invisible. How would you respond to her?

References

Gaunilo (1968). *The many-faced argument*. J. Hick and A. Gill (Eds.), New York: Macmillan.

Plantinga, A. (1974). *The nature of necessity*. Oxford: Oxford University Press.

St. Anselm (1958). Prologium, In *St. Anselm*. La Salle, IL: Open Court.

CHAPTER 5

The Problem of Divine Elusiveness

1. The Problem

God is elusive in that he is not readily perceptible to us. Why does he not show up in a TV station and declare to the world that he exists? If he does, everyone will believe in him and go to heaven. Given that he is omnibenevolent, he should show himself to us. However, he does not. It appears that he is not omnibenevolent, or that he does not exist.

Why is God elusive? This question raises a philosophical problem that might be called "the problem of divine elusiveness." Atheists' response to it is that he is invisible to us because he does not exist. However, this response is not available to theists, for if they avail themselves of it, they would cease to be theists. Consequently, theists have the burden of explaining why he is elusive. This chapter discusses how theists confront the burden.

2. Four Commonsensical Responses

The following four commonsensical responses to the problem of divine elusiveness are available to theists.

First, theists might suggest that we will see God, provided that we go through a long and arduous training. The training involves regularly going to church, praying to him, singing hymns, and doing other things that religious leaders, such as ministers and priests, tell us to do. Once we finish the training, we become religious experts and see him. In general, experts can see certain things that nonexperts cannot. For example, doctors can see a tumor in an X-ray image while ordinary people cannot. Wine connoisseurs can discriminate between wines of different brands while ordinary people cannot. Similarly, religious experts can see him while ordinary people cannot.

Second, theists might suggest that God wants us to believe in him despite the absence of perceptual evidence for his existence, i.e., although we cannot see him. We should believe in him by the leap of faith, i.e., we should jump to belief in him on insufficient evidence. On this account, he is testing us. Believing in him on faith means that we have passed the test, and that we will go to heaven. Disbelieving in him on the ground that we cannot see him means that we have failed the test, and that we will go to hell after we die.

Third, theists might suggest that God is elusive out of his respect for human beings' free will. He wants us to choose the belief of him over the disbelief of him, and he does not want to force the belief of him on us. If he came down to us and made himself visible to us, we would have no choice but to believe in him, and we would have no free will to choose between the belief and the disbelief of him. He does not want to deprive us of the free will to choose between the belief and the disbelief of him. By remaining elusive, he gives us the chance to exercise our free will and believe in him.

Fourth, theists might suggest that God is an infinite being while humans are finite beings, and thus that he transcends human comprehension, i.e., that he is incomprehensible to humans. Humans are to him as ants are to protons and black holes. Humans are not intelligent enough to understand why he is elusive any more than ants are intelligent enough to understand why protons and black holes are elusive.

All four of these theistic points might warrant a discussion of their unique and individual weaknesses and further support that can be given them. In the interest of saving space, I say only the following thing: if God showed up and proved to us that there are no other deities, such as Allah and Vishnu, there would be less religious war between the followers of different religions. Preventing religious war is more important than respecting our free will to kill heretics.

3. Panentheism

Theists might advance the view on God called "panentheism" to solve the problem of divine elusiveness. According to panentheism, God's body is the universe, and that his mind exists outside the universe. Harvey Cawdron states that panentheism "identifies the universe with the body of God and the part of God outside it with the mind" (Cawdron, 2021, p. 357).

Panentheists would say that God is not elusive, given that we see his body all the time. We see his body every day without knowing that we do. To use an analogy, our Paleolithic ancestors breathed oxygen in the air every day without knowing that they did. In the similar vein, Paul Moser states, "people may actually hear God through conscience without correctly identifying the 'voice' of conscience as God" (Moser, 2020, p. 191). Therefore, it is wrong to think that God is elusive.

4. Responses to Panentheism

Is panentheism an adequate response to the problem of divine elusiveness? A negative answer to this question is defended in this section.

The panentheistic notion of God is esoteric, i.e., it is far from the commonsensical notion of him found in the Bible. According to the Bible, he created Adam in his image, which implies that he looks like a human being, and that he is separate from the universe, i.e., he and the universe are separate entities, just as an apple and an orange are separate entities. According to panentheism, however, he and the universe are not separate entities, and the universe is part of him. So what? The panentheistic response to the problem of divine elusiveness comes with the cost of diverging from the ordinary conception of him.

Panentheists claim that when we see the universe, we see God's body. Objectors might say that we rather see a goblin's body. Alternatively, they might say that we rather see a gremlin's body.

It is not clear how we can resolve the dispute between panentheists and objectors.

According to the Big Bang theory, the universe was an infinitely small point called "a singularity" approximately 13.8 billion years ago, there was nothing before the Big Bang, and spacetime began to exist along with the Big Bang. If the Big Bang theory is true, God's body is approximately 13.8 billion years old. This consequence would not be agreeable to those who believe that it is impossible for his body not to exist, i.e., that his body is a necessary being. In addition, interesting questions arise. Where was his mind prior to the Big Bang? How old was his mind at the time of the Big Bang?

Panentheists might suggest that the Big Bang theory is false, that the universe is eternal, and that the universe does not have a beginning, i.e., that no one created God's body. This view on the universe goes hand in hand with Roger Penrose's (2012) conformal cyclic cosmology according to which the universe infinitely reiterates expansion and contraction, i.e., there were and will be infinitely many Big Bangs. Conformal cyclic cosmology and panentheism jointly imply that God's body infinitely reiterates expansion and contraction. A problem with this implication is that it is mysterious why his body expands and contracts infinitely many times. Why does he constantly change his body size?

Panentheism does not go well with the view that God created the universe. Panentheism and the view on him jointly imply that his mind created his body. Before the universe was created, only his mind existed, and his mind created his body. How can his mind create his body? It is inexplicable how such an event can occur. Accordingly, those who believe that he created the universe should not believe that the universe is his body.

Panentheism implies that a human being is part of God's body. However, a human body ultimately dies and decays. Why does part of his body die and decay? Moreover, I am made up of my body and mind. It makes sense to say that my body is part of his body, but it does not make sense to say that my mind is part of his body. How can my mind be part of a physical thing?

Panentheism implies that every part of the universe is part of God's body. It follows that every corner of the universe is holy, and we should pay respect to it. However, there are harmful things in the world. For example, Corona virus and heinous criminals are harmful to us. Moreover, there are dirty and ugly things in the world. We can see such things in bathrooms and sewers. Why are some parts of God's body harmful, dirty, and ugly? Should we pay homage to them? Panentheists owe us answers to these disconcerting questions.

5. Summary

Why is God elusive? Theists might suggest that we can see God provided that we become religious experts, that he wants us to believe in him on faith, that he only respects our free will to choose between belief and disbelief in him, and humans cannot understand why he is elusive.

Panentheists suggest that God is not elusive because the universe is his body and we see his body all the time. However, panentheism is far from the biblical conception of God. Moreover, panentheists owe us answers to the following perverse questions: Why not say that we see a goblin's body? Where was God's mind before the Big Bang? How can God's mind create his body? Is his body a contingent being? Why does he change his body size? Why do some parts of his body die and decay? Why are some parts of his body harmful, dirty and ugly?

Study Questions

1. Assess the four commonsensical responses to the problem of divine elusiveness in Section 2. Are the responses consistent with the view that God is omnibenevolent and omniscient?

2. Can panentheism be a solution to the problem of divine elusiveness? Why? Why not? Do you have an alternative response to the problem of divine elusiveness?

References

Cawdron, H. (2021). Getting to know a God you do not believe in: Panetheism, externalism, and divine hiddenness. *Zygon*, 56(2), 352-373.

Moser, P. (2020). Reply to Schellenberg. In M. and R. van Arragon (Eds.), *Contemporary debates in philosophy of religion*. Oxford: Wiley Blackwell.

Penrose, R. (2012). *Cycles of time: An extraordinary new view of the universe*. New York: Random House.

CHAPTER 6

The Origin of the Universe

1. Overview

Why does the universe exist? Where did it come from? Does it have a beginning and/or an end? Different answers to these questions can be found in the Bible and in the two scientific theories: the Big Bang theory and conformal cyclic cosmology (CCC). The Bible says, "In the beginning, God created the heavens and the earth" (Genesis, 1:1). Thus, God created the universe. The Big Bang theory claims that the universe began about 13.8 billion years ago. Thus, the universe has a beginning. CCC asserts that the universe infinitely reiterates expansion and contraction. Thus, the universe neither has a beginning nor an end. This chapter compares these rival accounts of the origin of the universe.

2. No Infinitely Many Years

The Big Bang theory holds that there was neither space nor time before the Big Bang, that the universe was an infinitely small point, and that it expanded at extremely high speed about 13.8 billion years ago. The Big Bang theory is reticent about the cause of the Big Bang.

Carlo Alvaro (2021, p. 9) claims that God triggered the Big Bang. He presents the following two interesting arguments to show that the world has a beginning. (i) It is impossible for an infinite number of years to have passed, and it is only possible for a finite number of years to have passed (Alvaro, 2021, p. 5). To put it differently, infinitely many years could not have gone, and only finitely many years could have gone. Consequently, if the world did not have a beginning, there would be no present. However, there is present. Therefore, the world has a beginning.

(ii) A contradiction can be derived from the idea that infinitely many years have flown, and thus infinitely many years could not have flown. Consider the set of infinitely many past years. Subtract all the even-numbered years from the set. The odd-numbered years would be left in the set. Accordingly, infinitely many years minus infinitely many years is infinitely many years. Now, subtract both all the even-numbered and odd-numbered years from the set. No year would be left in the set. Accordingly, infinitely many years minus infinitely many years is zero year. However, it is a contradiction to say that infinitely many years minus infinitely many years is both infinitely many years and zero year. Therefore, "the universe must be a collection composed of a finite number of years" (Alvaro, 2021, p. 6). In other words, finitely many years must have passed.

Any statement of the form "P and ~p" is a contradiction. For example, it is a contradiction that it is raining and not raining. A contradiction is false, and we do not need to observe the world to determine whether it is true or false. Even if we do not observe the world, we can know that it is false. Similarly, it is a contradiction that infinity minus infinity is both infinity and zero. Given that this contradiction can be derived from the statement that infinitely many years have passed, it is a contradiction that infinitely many years have passed. We do not need to observe the past to determine whether it is true or false that infinitely many years have passed. Even if we do not observe the past, we can know that it is false that infinitely many years have passed.

How do I respond to Alvaro's foregoing arguments? They have the following two implications that theists would find unacceptable (Park, forthcoming, Subsection 3.3). (1) The world must have an end. If there could not be infinitely many *past* years, there cannot be infinitely many *future* years, either. Consequently, God is not only the creator of the world but also the terminator of the world. It is not clear whether we should be thankful to him for terminating the world.

(2) Just as the world had a beginning and an end, so heaven and hell must have beginnings and ends. This implication conflicts with the popular religious view that believers and disbelievers will be sent to heaven and hell, respectively, after they die, and that they will stay there *forever*. Moreover, Alvaro faces the following disconcerting questions: Where do believers and disbelievers go, after heaven and hell cease to exist? Where does God go after the world is terminated? Will he be terminated along with the world?

3. Conformal Cyclic Cosmology

Roger Penrose (2012) advances CCC, according to which the

universe infinitely repeats the process of expansion and contraction, and that there were and will be infinitely many Big Bangs. On this account, the world neither has a beginning nor an end. CCC clashes with Alvaro's view that God triggered the Big Bang.

Alvaro raises an interesting objection to CCC, viz., CCC is incompatible with the second law of thermodynamics. The second law of thermodynamics holds that entropy tends to increase. A closed system, if left alone, tends to become disorderly as time passes, and it does not tend to become orderly. Suppose, for example, that a professor's office is orderly, and that it is left alone. As time passes, it will tend to become disorderly. An orderly office tends to become disorderly, but a disorderly office does not tend to become orderly. No energy is required for an orderly office to become disorderly, but energy is required for a disorderly office to become orderly. The same holds for the world. The world tends to become disorderly, i.e., the entropy of the world tends to increase. No energy is required for the orderly world to become disorderly, but energy is required for the disorderly world to become orderly. It follows that if the world does not have a beginning, it would be maximally disorderly now. However, it is not maximally disorderly now. Therefore, the world has a beginning, and God created it.

Alvaro's objection to CCC is forceful and penetrating. My response to it is to postulate the existence of a hitherto hidden mechanism because of which the entropy of the world drops from the maximum to minimum values right after each Big Bang.

According to cosmologists, the universe was so hot and dense right after the Big Bang that the laws of physics broke down, which implies that the second law of thermodynamics also broke down. It might be that a hitherto hidden mechanism operated during this early period of the universe, and as a result, the entropy dropped to the minimum value. I leave to scientists the task of finding the empirical evidence for this speculative assumption.

Theists' position and atheists' position compete with each other. Theists' position holds that God created the world. By contrast, atheists' position holds that the world has neither a beginning nor an end, which implies that it does not have a creator. There can be the following dialectics between a theist and an atheist:

> Atheist: "I reject your position God created the world because it conflicts with the first law of thermodynamics according to which mass-energy is conserved. How could God create the world out of nothing? How could he violate the first law of thermodynamics?"

> Theist: "God is omnipotent. So he could create the world out of nothing, and he could violate the first law of thermodynamics. By the way, I reject your position the universe doesn't have a beginning because it conflicts with the second law of thermodynamics."

Atheist: "There might be a hitherto hidden mechanism because of which the entropy of the world drops from the maximum to minimum values right after each Big Bang. By the way, I reject your view that God is eternal. How can he be infinitely many years old? A contradiction can be derived from your view that he is infinitely many years old. Therefore, he cannot be infinitely many years old."

Theist: "I similarly reject your view that the world is eternal. How can the world be infinitely many years old? A contradiction can be derived from your view that the world is infinitely many years old. The universe cannot be infinitely many years old."

In sum, theists' position conflicts with the first law of thermodynamics, and makes the ad hoc assumption that God exists. In addition, it is vulnerable to the charge that a contradiction can be derived from the idea that he is infinitely old. By contrast, atheists' position conflicts with the second law of thermodynamics, and makes the ad hoc assumption that the hitherto hidden mechanism operates right after each Big Bang. In addition, it is vulnerable to the charge that a contradiction can be derived from the idea that the world is infinitely old.

4. Summary

The Bible holds that God created the universe. The Big Bang theory holds that the universe began with the Big Bang. CCC holds that there were and will be infinitely many Big Bangs. Alvaro asserts that God triggered the Big Bang. The universe has a beginning because it is impossible for an infinite amount of time to have already passed and because a contradiction can be derived from the idea that an infinite amount of time has passed. I object that if an infinite amount of time cannot pass, the universe has an end, and so do heaven, hell, and God. There can be a debate between theists and atheists over whose position is better.

Study Questions

1. Alvaro argues that since many years could not have passed, the world has a beginning. Suppose that his argument is strong. What, then, becomes of heaven and hell? Can they be eternal? What about God? Can he be eternal?

2. Theists claim that God is infinitely old and created the world, while atheists claim that the world is infinitely old, and hence that the world does not have a creator. Whose position would you choose? Why?

References

Alvaro, C. (2021). Atheism as an extreme rejection of rational evidence for the existence of God. *The Heythrop Journal*, 62(2), 1-16.

Park, S. (forthcoming). Did God create the universe? *Cosmos and History*, (To be determined)

Penrose, R. (2012). *Cycles of time: An extraordinary new view of the universe*. New York: Random House.

7 CHAPTER

The Problems of Divine Location and Age

1. Introduction

The Bible states, "In the beginning, God created the heavens and the earth" (Genesis 1:1). The argument from design also implies that he created the world, as noted in Section 2 of Chapter 3 chapter. In this chapter, I introduce two philosophical problems that I call "the problems of divine location and age" against the view that he created the world.

2. The Problem Divine Location

The contention that God created the world is puzzling and invites the following perverse question. Where did he exist before he created the world? Theists might suggest that he existed in heaven. This suggestion, however, only prompts a further question. Where did he exist before he created heaven? These questions create a philosophical problem that I call "the problem of divine location" according to which "it is not clear where God existed before he created the Universe" (Park, 2017, p. 162).

The Big Bang theory holds that the universe began about 13.8 billion years ago with the Big Bang, and that there was nothing before the Big Bang. There was even no space before the Big Bang, so it appears that God did not exist before the Big Bang. After all, to say that he existed in no place before the Big Bang indicates that he did not exist. In general, if an object exists at all, it exists in a certain place, i.e., an object needs space in order to exist. It follows that if space does not exist, no object can exist, and that since space did not exist before the Big Bang, he could not exist before the Big Bang.

How might theists attempt to solve the problem of divine location? They might suggest that God existed outside of space, i.e., he existed in the nonspatial realm before he created the universe. On this account, it is wrong to think that an object needs space in order to exist. To put it differently, an object can exist even if there is no space.

This intriguing suggestion, however, invites the following three objections. First, who created the nonspatial realm? Theists would answer that God created it. But a new question arises. Where was he before he created the nonspatial realm? Thus, we are back to the problem of divine location (Park, 2017, p. 168).

Second, to say that an object exists outside of space means that it does not have a shape, a size, and a length. If God had existed in the nonspatial realm before the Big Bang, he must not have had a shape, a size, and a length. It is not clear how such a being could create the universe. Theists can reply that since he was omnipotent, he could create the world, although he did not have a shape, a size, and a length.

Third, the suggestion that God did not have a shape, a size, and a length before the Big Bang clashes with what the Bible says. According to the Bible, he created Adam and Eve in his image, which indicates that he has a shape, a size, and a length. Theists can retort that before the Big Bang, he did not have a shape, a size, and a length, but that after the Big Bang, he acquired the physical properties.

Theists might suggest that God and the world came into being simultaneously. On this account, he came into existence along with the Big Bang, but he did not exist before the Big Bang. Since he did not exist before the Big Bang, it is wrong to ask where he was before he created the world.

An immediate objection to this suggestion is that it is mysterious how God could create the world when he and the world came into being simultaneously. In general, a creator exists prior to the thing that he creates. For example, a watchmaker exists and then a watch exists. It is implausible that a watchmaker and a watch pop into existence at the same time. Similarly, it is implausible that God and the world popped into existence simultaneously (Park, 2017, p. 164). Theists, however, can again invoke his omnipotence to diffuse this objection, saying that he can do anything, so he could create the world while he was in the process of being created.

Theists might argue that an object can exist even if we cannot talk about its location. For example, the universe exists, but we cannot talk about its location. We cannot because it is all that there is, i.e., because there is no bigger object which embeds the universe. To use an analogy, we can talk about the location of Ulsan because there is a bigger object, e.g., South Korea, which embeds Ulsan. When asked where Ulsan is located, we can say that it is in the southeast of South Korea. By contrast, the universe is not part of a bigger object, so we cannot talk about its location. Theists might claim that before the Big Bang, there was God and nothing else, i.e., he was all that there was, and thus that we cannot talk about his location. In sum, just as it is wrong to ask where the universe is located, so it is wrong to ask where he was located before the Big Bang (Park, 2017, p. 163).

3. The Problem of Divine Age

The contention that God created the world is puzzling in another respect and invites the following perverse question. How old was he when he created the world? This question leads to a philosophical problem that I call "the problem of divine age," according to which "it is not clear how old God was when He created the Universe" (Park, 2017, p. 164).

Some theists might suggest that God is eternal, which implies that he was infinitely old at the time of the Big Bang. This suggestion, however, is at variance with the Big Bang theory according to which time came to exist along with the Big Bang, which implies that there was no time before the Big Bang, which in turn implies that it was impossible for God to be infinitely old before the Big Bang. In general, to say that an object exists in no time indicates that it does not exist.* For example, to say that

---

* See Park (2023) for a critical discussion of the view that God is an abstract entity.

Alexander the Great existed in no time in the human history means that he did not exist in the human history. Analogously, to say that God existed in no time before the Big Bang means that he did not exist before the Big Bang. If something exists at all, it exists in time, i.e., an object needs time to exist.

However, theists might insist that God existed in the nontemporal realm until he created the universe. I set aside the issue of who created the nontemporal realm. I instead raise the following objection. In the absence of time, he would be frozen, and he could not do anything. He could not even move his finger. After all, moving a finger means that a finger was in a certain place at t_1, and that it was in another place at t_2, which in turn implies that time flew from t_1 to t_2. In other words, moving a finger requires the passage of time (Park, 2017, p. 164).

Let me add that if God exists in the nontemporal realm, he cannot escape from it. To say that he gets out of the nontemporal realm means that he was in the nontemporal realm at t_1 and he is out of the nontemporal realm at t_2, which in turn means that time lapsed from t_1 to t_2. The lapse of time is required for him to get out of the nontemporal realm. However, time does not pass in the nontemporal realm. Therefore, he cannot get out of the nontemporal realm. Therefore, he is locked up in the nontemporal realm forever, and he can do nothing in the nontemporal realm.

Theists might now suggest that God and the world came into being simultaneously, so he was zero year old when he created the world. A problem with this suggestion is that it implies that he did not exist before the beginning of the universe, and hence that it does not go well with the view that he is a necessary being, i.e., with the view that it is impossible for he not to exist. When challenged to answer who created him, some theists answer that he is a necessary being, so nobody created him. They cannot give such an answer, if they claim that he and the world came into being simultaneously.

In the face of the preceding discussion, theists might now reject the old hypothesis that time did not exist before the Big Bang, and propose the new hypothesis that time existed before the Big Bang, and that before the Big Bang an infinite amount of time passed. On the new hypothesis, he was infinitely old at the time of the Big Bang.

A problem with this new hypothesis is that it relies on the substantival conception of time. According to the substantival conception of time, time is independent of the motions of physical objects, so time can flow even if all physical objects stop moving. Under the relational conception of time, however, time is dependent upon the state of motion, and time does not flow in the absence of motion (Kosso, 1998, p. 35). Before the Big Bang, no physical object exited, so there was no motion, and time did not pass (Park, 2017, p. 165).

Theists might now suggest that God has a body, a physical object, just like a human, that his body existed before the Big Bang, that there were motions in his body, so time passed before the Big Bang, and that he was infinitely old when the Big Bang occurred. This new suggestion is compatible with the relational conception of time.

This new suggestion, however, invites the objection: where was his body before the Big Bang? Moreover, it clashes with the second law of thermodynamics according to which entropy tends to increase in a closed system, i.e., if a system is left alone, it tends to become disorderly, and energy from outside is required to make it orderly. There was nothing but God before the Big Bang, so entropy must have been increasing in his body until the Big Bang occurred. Given that an infinite amount of time flew prior to the Big Bang, his body must have been infinitely disorderly. How could he create the universe when his body was infinitely disorderly? (Park, 2017, p. 166)

4. Summary

Theists might suggest, to solve the problem of divine location, that God exists outside of space. However, this suggestion invites the question of who created the nonspatial realm, the question of how a nonspatial being could create the universe, and the question of how we can reconcile it with the conception of him in the Bible. Theists might suggest that he and the world came into being simultaneously, and that just because we cannot talk about his location, it does not follow that he does not exist.

Theists might suggest, to solve the problem of divine age, that God was infinitely old. However, this suggestion invites the objection that time did not flow before the Big Bang, so it was impossible for him to be infinitely old. Theists might suggest that he exists outside of time. This suggestion invites the question of who created the nontemporal realm, and the objection that he can do nothing in the nontemporal realm. Theists might suggest that he and the world came into being simultaneously. However, this suggestion conflicts with the view that he is a necessary being. On the substantival conception of time, time passes even if no change occurs. On the relational conception of time, by contrast, time does not pass if no change occurs.

Study Questions

1. What is the problem of divine location? State and evaluate theists' possible responses to the problem of divine location.

2. What is the problem of divine age? State and assess theists' possible responses to the problem of divine location.

References

Kosso, Peter (1998). Appearance and reality: Introduction to the philosophy of physics. Oxford: Oxford University Press.

Park, S. (2017). The problems of divine location and age. *European Journal of Science and Theology*, 13(2), 161-170.

Park, S. (2023). Is God an abstract entity? *European Journal of Science and Theology*, 19(4), 71-81.

CHAPTER 8

The Problem of Divine Foreknowledge

1. Overview

There is a conflict between the view that God is omniscient and the view that we have free will. It appears that if he knew what you would do, you have no choice but to do what he already knew you would do. It appears that if you have free will do to something or not to do it, he did not know what you would do. This conflict is known as the problem of divine foreknowledge. Boethius (466–524) and Ockham (1287–1347) grappled with this problem. We will evaluate their attempts to solve it in this chapter.

2. The Conflict

A past event seems to be unalterable. For example, it is a past event that Caesar crossed the Rubicon in 49 BC. We cannot do anything now to change this past event. No matter what we do now, we cannot replace it with a new past event that Caesar did not cross the Rubicon. Once an event occurred, it is permanently fixed, and it is not subject to change.

God is omniscient, which implies that he *knew* everything that you would do even before you were born. Suppose, for example, that when you were a high school student, you applied for UNIST and MIT, that you got the admissions from both universities, that you deliberated on which one to choose, and that you chose UNIST over MIT. Even before you made this choice, he knew that you would make this choice. Therefore, you could not but make this choice, i.e., you did not have the free will to choose MIT.

No one forced you to choose UNIST over MIT, so you may strongly believe that you exercised your free will when you chose UNIST, i.e., that you had the ability to choose the MIT when you chose UNIST. To say so, however, means that you had the ability to change the past state of affairs that God knew that you would choose UNIST. To state it differently, to say so means that you had the ability to replace (U) with (M):

(U) God knew that you would choose UNIST.
(M) God knew that you would choose MIT.

However, you did not have the ability to replace (U) with (M) when you chose UNIST. Why not? As we noted earlier, past states of affairs, including (U), were permanently fixed, and they are not alterable. Therefore, you did not have the ability to replace (U) with (M), i.e., you could not choose MIT and could not but choose UNIST.

The preceding discussion shows that there is a conflict between divine foreknowledge and human free will. It appears that if God knew beforehand what you would do, you do not have the free will to do otherwise, and that if you have the free will to do otherwise, he did not know what you would do. If he did not know what you would do, however, he is not omniscient, and the omniscient being does not exist. In sum, the conflict between divine foreknowledge and human free will seems to show that he does not exist. This problem is called "the problem of divine foreknowledge."

The problem of foreknowledge does not claim that God *forces* you to make a certain choice, nor does it claim that he *controls* you. It rather claims that you make a choice as he already knew you would, i.e., that you behave exactly as he foresaw you would. To say that you have free will implies that you have the ability to change the past state of affairs that he knew in advance what you would do, but it is impossible for you to change that past state of affairs. Therefore, you do not have free will.

3. Boethius

Boethius's response to the problem of divine foreknowledge is to argue that God exists outside of time (Boethius, 1962). Since he exists outside of time, it is false that he *knew* what you would do, and that there is a conflict between divine foreknowledge and human free will. On Boethius's account, even if God exists in the timeless realm, he is omniscient and knows everything that you did, do, and will do. In the timeless realm, he observes all the past, present, and future events.

What are we to make of Boethius's response to the problem of divine foreknowledge? If God exists outside of time, he is frozen. As a consequence, there can be no change in him, i.e., a change cannot occur in him. Suppose that he has a body. Can he move his body? The answer is "No." The motion of his body is a kind of change, and a change cannot occur in him. Suppose that he has a mind. Can he think? The answer is "No." Thinking is a kind of change, and a change cannot occur in him. Can he observe all the past, present, and future events? The answer is "No." Observing is a kind of change, and a change cannot occur in him.

Moreover, Boethius has merely replaced a problem with another. A state of affairs in the timeless realm is not alterable any more than a state of affairs in the past is alterable. After all, time does not pass in the timeless realm, so change cannot occur there. Suppose that you are a UNIST student, and that you ponder whether to get a job or to go to graduate school after you graduate from UNIST. If God knows in the timeless realm that you will get a job, you do not have the free will to go to graduate school. You will just do exactly what he knows you will do, i.e., you will get a job. To say that you have the free will to go to graduate school means that you have the ability to replace (J) with (G).

(J) In the timeless realm, God knows that you will get a job.
(G) In the timeless realm, God knows that you will go to graduate school.

You do not have the ability to replace (J) with (G) because change cannot occur in the timeless realm (Park, 2017, p. 164).

In sum, Boethius dispels an old objection: A past state of affairs is not alterable, so we do not have free will. However, he invites a new objection: A state of affairs in the timeless realm is not alterable, so we do not have free will.

4. Ockham

Ockham's response to the problem of divine foreknowledge is to argue that we can change some past events, although we cannot change other past events (Ockham, 1983). For example, we cannot change the past event that Caesar crossed the Rubicon, nor can we change the past state of affairs that God knew that Caesar would cross the Rubicon. But we can change the past state of affairs that he knew what we would do. Suppose that you are a UNIST student. You contemplate over whether to get a job or to go to graduate school. He knew that you would get a job. It is a past state of affairs that he knew that you would get a job. However, you can change it by choosing to go to graduate school. Your going to graduate school means that you replace (P1) with (P2):

(P1) God knew that you would get a job.
(P2) God knew that you would go to graduate school.

Before you go to graduate school, (P1) was a past state of affairs. The moment you go to graduate school, however, (P1) is replaced with (P2), i.e., (P1) ceases to be a past state of affairs, and (P2) becomes a past state of affairs. Consequently, it does not matter whether you get a job or go to graduate school. God knew what you would do. If you get a job, he knew that you would get a job. If you go to graduate school, he knew that you would go to graduate school. In sum, whatever you do, he knew what you would do.

Ockham's suggestion implies that we can never know whether God knew in advance what you would do in the future. Suppose again that you are a UNIST student, and that you mull over whether to get a job or to go to graduate school. Before you made the decision, we can never know whether God knew what you would choose to do. After you get a job, we can know that he knew that you would get a job. After you go to graduate school, we can know that he knew that you would go to graduate school. Before you make the choice, however, we cannot know whether he knew that you would get a job or go to graduate school. In sum, skepticism about his past mental states is in the offing, i.e., we cannot know what happened in his mind regarding your career until you make a choice.

Ockham's suggestion can be reduced to absurdity. Suppose that a weather forecaster predicts that it will rain tomorrow. A day passes, and it is sunny, contrary to what the forecaster predicted. People blame the forecaster for having made a false prediction. To their surprise, however, the forecaster replies that a few hours after she made the prediction, the old future state of affairs that it will rain was replaced with the new future state of affairs that it will be sunny. Therefore, her prediction was true. On her account, just as a past state of affairs can be replaced with another past state of affairs, so a future state of affair can be replaced with another future state of affairs. Whenever her prediction turns out to be false, she claims that an old future state of affairs was replaced with a new future state of affairs, and that every prediction of hers is true. This defense of the prediction is absurd. By parity of reasoning, Ockham's defense of divine foreknowledge is also absurd.

5. Summary

The problem of divine foreknowledge states that divine foreknowledge conflicts with human free will. If he knew what you would do, you have no choice but to do what he knew you would do. Boethius's response is to argue that he exists outside of time. In the timeless realm, he knows everything that you will do. A problem with this response is that change cannot occur in the timeless realm, and thus that human free will cannot change God's knowledge about what you would do. Ockham's response is to argue that human free will can change God's past mental state. Human free will has the ability to replace a past fact that he knew that you would do something with another past fact that he knew that you would do something else. In the similar vein, however, whenever a weather forecaster makes a false prediction about tomorrow's weather, she might argue absurdly that a future event that she predicted would occur was replaced with a new future event that actually occurred.

Study Questions

1. Explicate the problem of divine foreknowledge, and then Boethius's response to it. Do you accept or reject his response? Why? Can God have free will and know in advance what he will do? In other words, is divine foreknowledge compatible or incompatible with divine free will?

2. Explicate the problem of divine foreknowledge, and then Ockham's response to it. Imagine that 100 years ago, God had a conversation with an angel about your career. The angel asked he about what you would do. He answered that you would get a job as opposed to go to graduate school. What if you choose to go to graduate school? What would become of the conversation between him and the angel? How would Ockham answer this question? Do you accept or reject his answer? Why?

References

Boethius (1962). *The consolation of philosophy*, prose VII, trans. Richard Green, New York: The Bobbs-Merrill Company.

Ockham (1983). *Predestination, God's foreknowledge, and future contingents*. 2nd ed., Hackett Publishing Company.

Park, S. (2017). The problems of divine location and age. *European Journal of Science and Theology*, 13(2), 161-170.

CHAPTER

9

The Problem of Evil

1. The Content

Evil exists in the world. Typical examples of evil are murder, rape, floods, earthquakes, and cancer. Murder and rape are human evil, given that they are caused by humans. By contrast, floods, earthquakes, and cancer are natural evil, given that they are caused by nature. Evil, whether human or natural, can be defined as that which causes pain to humans.

The problem of evil states that God and evil cannot exist simultaneously, that evil exists, and thus that he does not exist. Epicurus (342–270 B.C.) formulates the problem of evil as follows:

> Is God willing to prevent evil, but not able? Then he is not omnipotent. Is he able, but not willing? Then he is malevolent. Is he both able and willing? Then from whence comes evil? (Hume, 1779/1998, p. 63)

God is omnipotent, so he must have the ability to destroy evil. He is omniscient, so he must know that evil exists. He is omnibenevolent, so he must not tolerate evil. If so, why does evil exist? The existence of evil seems to show that the supernatural entity that allegedly has the three properties does not exist.

2. Theist Responses

Stephen Wykstra (1984) writes that evil is outweighed by good, and that we cannot know about good which is greater than evil. To use an analogy, suppose that a child got a cold. His mother gives him the medicine, and the medicine tastes bitter to the child. The child thinks that the medicine is evil. The child does not understand why his mother inflicts pain to him. Similarly, murder, rape, earthquakes, and floods inflict pain on humans. Greater good, however, will come out of these evil things. We are finitely intelligent, so we cannot know about greater good. By contrast, God is infinitely intelligent, so he knows about greater good.

John Hick (1966) opines that evil helps us to improve ourselves. After we experience trials and tribulations, we become strong, mature, and virtuous. Suppose, for example, that you grow up in a poor family. You experience hunger at home and humiliation in school. As a result, you work hard in school, get admission from UNIST, graduate with a high GPA, and get a good job. As this example indicates, hardship and adversity make humans intellectually mature and economically better.

St. Augustine (354–430) suggests that evil exists due to human free will, and that God only respects human free will. Human evil, such as murder and rape, are caused by human free will. Without perpetrators' free will, there would be no human evil. We should not blame God for the existence of human evil.

How about natural evil, such as drought and famine? According to the Bible, they are caused by Adam and Eve's free will in the Garden of Eden. They chose to eat the fruit from the tree of knowledge, although God told them not to do so. As a result, they were deported from the Garden of Eden, and their descendants suffer from natural evil. St. Augustine might add that some people die of natural disasters, such as drought and flood, because they chose to live in the unlucky areas. Their bad choice is responsible for their suffering.

Some theists might suggest that evil does not exist. What appears to be evil to us is good to God. His conception of good and evil is different from humans' conception of good and evil. We think that droughts, plagues, and murder are evil. However, he thinks that they are good. He and humans have different eyes, so to speak. Since evil does not exist, the problem of evil is misguided, and we can maintain the belief that he exists.

Some theists might suggest that God is a transcendental being, i.e., that he transcends human comprehension. He is an infinite being, whereas humans are finite beings. The finite beings' minds are not powerful enough to understand the infinite being any more than ants' minds are powerful enough to understand humans. It is a manifestation of arrogance for humans to try to understand why he does not do anything to evil.

Some theists might suggest that evil is necessary for the existence of good, i.e., without evil, good cannot exist. Darkness is necessary for the existence of brightness, i.e., without darkness, brightness cannot exist. Without hatred, there cannot be love. Without war, there cannot be peace. Without the shortage of food, there cannot be the abundance of food. So some theists might claim.

Some theists might suggest that God is not omnibenevolent. He knows that humans suffer from evil, but he does not destroy evil because he does not love humans. The best thing that humans can do under such circumstances is to worship him harder so that he might be less angry at us. If we are angry at him for not destroying evil, he will be angrier at us, and we will suffer more from evil.

3. Summary

The problem of evil states that the existence of God is incompatible with the existence of evil. Wykstra's response is to argue that there is a greater good behind evil, and that we do not know about it. Hick's response is to argue that evil makes us mentally mature. St. Augustine's response is to argue that human free will is the cause of evil. Other theists might say that evil does not exist, that we cannot understand God, that evil is necessary for the existence of good, and that he is not omnibenevolent. All these theist responses are subject to dispute.

Study Questions

1. What is the problem of evil? How do you evaluate Wykstra's response that evil is outweighed by good which we cannot know about, and

to Hick's response that evil is necessary to improve ourselves?

2. What is the problem of evil? How do you assess St. Augustine's response that evil exists due to human free will? How do you respond to the following suggestions? What appears to be evil to us is good to God. We cannot understand why he does not do anything to evil. Without evil, there could be no good. He is not omnibenevolent.

References

Hick, J. (1966). *Evil and the God of love*. New York: Harper and Tow.

Hume, D. (1779/1998). *Dialogues concerning natural religion*. Indianapolis: Hackett.

Wykstra, S. (1984). The Humean obstacle to evidential arguments from suffering: On avoiding the evils of appearance. *International Journal for the Philosophy of Religion* 16(2), 73-93.

CHAPTER

10

The Argument from Other Minds

1. Introduction

Alvin Plantinga (1967/1990), an eminent philosopher of religion, admits that the traditional arguments for the existence of God, such as the argument from design and the argument from miracles, are weak. Nonetheless, he argues, we can believe in God. He has put forward a famous argument for the belief of God that might be called "the argument from other minds." This chapter aims to analyze and criticize it.

2. The Argument from Other Minds

In this section, I introduce Plantinga's argument from other minds.

We can observe other people's bodies, but not their minds. For example, we can observe their bodily damage, but not their pain. We can observe their tears, but not their sorrow. Yet, we (can justifiably) believe that they have minds. We do not say that other people do not have minds on the ground that we cannot observe their minds. In short, we (can justifiably) believe that other people have minds, although we cannot observe their minds.

The same holds for God, according to Plantinga. Just as we can justifiably believe that other people have minds although we cannot observe their minds, so we can justifiably believe that God exists although we cannot observe him. We should not say that he does not exist because we cannot observe him. If we cannot believe that he exists because we cannot see him, we should not believe either that other people have minds because we cannot see their minds. In short, belief in God and belief in other minds are in the same boat.

3. Critical Responses

3.1. Reductio ad Absurdum

In this subsection, I run a reductio ad absurdum against Plantinga's argument from other minds, i.e., I show that it is absurd by deriving an absurd consequence from it.

Recall that Plantinga runs the following argument for the belief of God:

> (G) Just as we can justifiably believe that other people have minds, so we can justifiably believe that God exists.

What are we to make of this argument? In my view, it is similar to the following fallacious argument for the belief of a dragon:

> (D) Just as we can justifiably believe that other people have minds, so we can justifiably believe that a dragon exists.

"A dragon" in (D) can be replaced with "the flying spaghetti monster," "a pink elephant," "a goblin," "a ghost," "Santa Clause," and "a perfect spouse." If (D) is a bad argument, (G) is also a bad argument. (D) is a bad argument. Therefore, (G) is also a bad argument, pace Plantinga.

If Plantinga says that (G) is a good argument while (D) is a bad argument, he has the burden of pointing out a relevant difference between God and a dragon that would entitle him to say so. For now, it is not clear what the relevant difference between them is.

3.2. The Plurality of Religions

There are many religions in the world. How would the believers of other religions, say, Muslims and Hinduists, respond to Plantinga's argument, (G)?

Muslims would say that just as we believe that other people have minds, so we can believe that Allah exists. Analogously, Hinduists would say that just as we can believe that other people have minds, so we can believe that Vishnu exists. Thus, Christians, Muslims, and Hinduists would draw different conclusions from the same premise that we can believe that other people have minds.

An interesting question arises. Are all the three groups of religious believers – Christians, Muslims, and Hinduists – right to draw their conclusions? Or are only Christians right to draw their conclusion? Plantinga owes us an answer to this question because he draws the conclusion that God exists.

33. In the Same Boat?

Plantinga claims that belief in God and belief in other minds are in the same boat. In this section, I object that we have a good argument for the existence of other minds, but not for the existence of God.

Suppose that scientists develop a vaccine to conquer an epidemic. They apply it to white mice. It turns out that it works on them. They infer that it will also work on humans. Their inference can be reconstructed as follows:

White mice and humans are physiologically similar to each other.
The vaccine worked on white mice.
∴ It will also work on humans.

This argument is cogent, i.e., the premises are true, and the conclusion probably follows from them. Admittedly, we cannot rule out the possibility that a vaccine will not work on humans. However, it is likely that it will work on humans. Scientists construct such arguments all the time when they do science.

We can similarly construct the following argument to show that other people have minds:

You and I are physiologically similar to each other.

I feel pain when my body is injured.
∴ You feel pain too when your body is injured.

This argument is cogent just like the argument about a vaccine above. Admittedly, I cannot rule out the possibility that you are a sophisticated robot, i.e., that you do not have a mind. However, it is likely that you have a mind.

Can we construct a similar argument for the existence of God? We can construct the following argument on behalf of Plantinga:

God and other minds are similar to each other.
Other minds exist.
∴ God exists.

An interesting issue is whether the first premise is true. What would be the reason for thinking that it is true? Plantinga owe us an answer to this question. In the absence of an answer to this question, we can conclude that belief in God and belief in other minds are in different boats. Specifically, it is plausible that other people have minds, but it is dubious that God exists.

4. Summary

Plantinga claims that just as we believe that others have minds, so we can believe that God exists. Critics can raise the following objections. Dragon worshipers might claim that just as we believe that others have minds, so we can believe that a dragon exists. Muslims might claim that just as we believe that others have minds, so we can believe that Allah exists. Contrary to what Plantinga claims, we have a cogent argument for the existence of other minds, but not for the existence of God.

Study Questions

1. State Plantinga's argument for the belief of God. Put yourself in Plantinga's position and reply to the following objection. If (G) is a bad argument, (D) is also a bad argument. (D) is a bad argument. Therefore, (G) is also a bad argument.

2. Are all the three groups of religious believers (Christians, Muslims, and Hinduists) right to draw their conclusions? Or are only Christians right to draw their conclusion? Is Plantinga right to say that the belief of other minds and the belief of God are in the same boat?

Reference

Plantinga, A. (1967/1990). *God and other minds: A study of the rational justification of belief in God*. Ithaca: Cornell University Press.

CHAPTER 11

Religious Beliefs and Truths

1. Overview

Believers typically claim that we can accept religious claims on faith, and that if we passionately believe that God exists, it is true that he exists, i.e., that our passion makes the religious belief true. These views on religious beliefs and truths originate from two religious thinkers: Thomas Aquinas (1225–1274) and Søren Kierkegaard (1813–1855). This chapter critically examines their views on religious beliefs and truths.

2. Aquinas

We usually believe something on reason, i.e., we usually form a belief, provided that we have good evidence for it. For example, we believe that dinosaurs existed because we observed the fossils of dinosaurs. Without the fossil evidence, we would not believe that dinosaurs existed. To take another example, the police believe that a culprit committed a crime because they acquired the fingerprint evidence. Without the evidence, the police would not believe that the suspect committed a crime. These two examples indicate that we hold secular beliefs on sufficient evidence.

How about religious beliefs? Should we also hold religious beliefs on reason? Aquinas's answer is "No." According to him, some truths about God "exceed all the ability of human reason," that "we may accept them freely on faith" (Rowe, 2007, p. 93). We may believe, for example, that God exists by the leap of faith. To state it differently, we can jump to the conclusion that he exists on insufficient evidence or on no evidence.

How should we evaluate the act of believing in God on faith? Aquinas answers that "the believer's act of faith may be a meritorious deed" (Rowe, 2007, p. 93). In other words, it is praiseworthy to hold religious beliefs in the absence of evidence for them, and God will reward us for holding religious beliefs on faith. By contrast, it is blameworthy to lose faith. To lose faith is to disbelieve in him after believing in him. Those who lost faith are called "apostates," and they are despised in the theist community.

Is Aquinas's view on faith tenable? Let me make two critical comments on it. First, different religions worship different deities. Which deity should we choose? By the leap of faith, Christians, Muslims, and Hinduists believe in God, Allah, and Vishnu, respectively. Who are right? Why? Some people might even believe that a goblin exists by the leap of faith, and claim that it is praiseworthy to believe in a goblin.

Second, suppose that theists believe in God on faith, but that atheists disbelieve in him on what I call "maith" (Park, 2016, p. 59). Maith is the opposite of faith, whatever it is. We may freely disbelieve in him on maith. It is meritorious for atheists to disbelieve in God by the leap of maith. It is blameworthy to lose maith. To lose maith is to believe in him after disbelieving in him. Those who lost maith might be called "amostates," and they should be despised in the atheist community.

Theists would object that we "hold certain beliefs despite the lack of sufficient evidence for them all the time" (Park, 2021, p. 36). For example, we are under the cognitive illusion called "illusory superiority" (Hoorens, 1993). We believe that we are more intelligent than average, we drive better than average, we look better than average, etc. These beliefs are false but useful. We are happy when we maintain them, and unhappy when we form the true beliefs that we are less intelligent than average, we drive worse than average, and we look worse than average. The true beliefs only hurt our self-esteem, and as a result we might suffer from depression.

Just as we tend to overestimate ourselves, so scientists tend to overestimate their own theories. They believe that their theories are true despite the counterevidence against them. At the end of the 19th century, for example, scientists observed the perihelion motion of Mercury, i.e., the rotation of the orbit of Mercury. Newton's mechanics could not explain it, but scientists did not give up Newton's mechanics, and they dogmatically stuck to it. They had the faith in it, so to speak.

Alvin Plantinga (1967/1990) would offer a different example to show that we believe something despite the lack of sufficient evidence for it. He opines, as noted in Chapter 10, that we believe that others have minds although we do not have sufficient evidence for the existence of their minds. We can observe others' bodies, but not their minds. It follows that we do not have sufficient evidence for the existence for their minds, although we have sufficient evidence for the existence of their bodies.

Theists would suggest that we have faith in ourselves, scientists have faith in their theories, and we have faith in other minds. If it is rational to have faith in ourselves, in scientific theories, and in other minds, it is also rational to have faith in God. There is no reason for thinking that it is rational to have faith in ourselves, in scientific theories, and in other minds, but it is irrational to have faith in him.

3. Kierkegaard

Kierkegaard admits that there is no good evidence for religious beliefs, so they are absurd. However, if religious beliefs are passionately held, they are true. He says, "An objective uncertainty held fast in an appropriation-process of the most passionate inwardness is the truth, the highest truth attainable for an existing individual" (Kierkegaard, 1941, p. 182). For example, if you passionately believe that God exists, it is true that he exists. On this account, passion is the truth-maker for religious beliefs, i.e., passion makes religious beliefs true.

Kierkegaard would not say that passion makes even nonreligious beliefs true. For example, even if you passionately believe that the earth is flat, it is false that the earth is flat, and passion does not make it true that the earth is flat. To take another example, even if a lawyer passionately believes that his client, a serial killer, is not guilty, it is false that his client is not guilty. Religious beliefs, however, are different from nonreligious beliefs in that passion makes religious beliefs true, but not nonreligious beliefs. If you passionately believe that God loves you, it is true that he loves you.

In addition, Kierkegaard asserts that it is admirable to believe in God passionately in the absence of evidence. It is commendable and praiseworthy that you believe in him passionately, despite the absence of evidence for the belief of him. By contrast, it is reprehensible and blameworthy to lose the belief of him on the ground that there is no evidence for it. In short, those who adhere to the belief of him are virtuous, and those who lose the belief of him are vicious.

What are we to make of Kierkegaard's view on religious beliefs and truths? Let me make the following four critical comments. (i) Suppose that theists passionately believe that God exists, but atheists passionately believe that he does not. If Kierkegaard is right, theists' passion makes their belief true while atheists' passion makes their disbelief true. But it is impossible that theists' belief and atheists' disbelief are true, i.e., it is impossible that God exists and does not exist. Therefore, Kierkegaard's theory of religious beliefs and truths is false.

(ii) How should we respond to the suggestion that if a religious belief is passionately held, then it is true, but even if a nonreligious belief is passionately held, it might be false? The suggestion requires a strict distinction between religious and nonreligious beliefs, but there is no such distinction. Consider a tricky example: "Love your neighbors." Is this belief religious or nonreligious? Although it is from the Bible, there is nothing religious about it. Consider another tricky example: "A god and a human love each other." Although a god figures in this belief, a human also figures in it, so the belief is half-religious and half-secular. However, it does not make sense to say that if the belief is passionately held, it is half-true.

(iii) How would God respond to Kierkegaard's the suggestion that if a religious belief is passionately held, then it is true? He would reject it on the ground that it has the following absurd consequence. Imagine that Kierkegaard says to him, "God, you exist because I passionately believe you exist. You would cease to exist the moment I stop passionately believing you exist. Thus, you come into being and go out of being depending whether I passionately believe you exist." God will only say to Kierkegaard, "Are you serious?"

(iv) We should not conflate what Aristotle means by "true" with what Kierkegaard means by "true." Suppose that Aristotle says, "It is true that God exists." What he means is that the belief that God exists corresponds to reality, i.e., he exists (Section 2 of Chapter 1). In contrast, suppose that Kierkegaard says, "It is true that God exists." What he means is not that the belief corresponds to reality but rather that he passionately believes that God exists. It is one thing that he passionately believes that God exists. It is entirely another that he exists. In sum, when Kierkegaard says, "It is true that God exists," we should interpret his sentence not as asserting that God exists but rather as asserting that he passionately believes that God exists.

4. Summary

Aquinas claims that it is praiseworthy to have faith in God. However, believers of different religions have faith on different deities, and atheists have the maith that he does not exist. Theists would reply that it is rational to believe in him on insufficient evidence, just as it is rational for us to overestimate ourselves, just as it is rational for scientists to overestimate their pet theories, and just as it is rational to believe that others have minds.

Kierkegaard claims that a religious belief is true if and only if it is passionately held. Atheists would object that they passionately disbelieve that God exists. Kierkegaard asserts that passion makes religious beliefs true, but not nonreligious beliefs. However, there is no strict distinction between religious and nonreligious beliefs. God would be upset to hear from Kierkegaard that Kierkeggard's passion makes God exist. Aristotle would say that a religious belief is true not when it is passionately held but when it corresponds to reality.

Study Questions

1. What is the difference between believing something on reason and believing something on faith? Aquinas claims that we can believe in God by the leap of faith. How do you respond to him? Is it rational to hold religious beliefs on insufficient evidence? Why? Why not?

2. According to Kierkegaard, if a religious belief is passionately held, it is true. How would Aristotle respond to Kierkegaard? Aristotle espouses the correspondence theory of truth according to which a belief is true when it corresponds to reality. Who do you agree with? Why? Is it admirable or not to believe in God in the absence of evidence? Why?

References

Hoorens, V. (1993). Self-enhancement and superiority biases in social comparison. *European Review of Social Psychology*, 4 (1), 113-139.

Kierkegaard, S. (1941). *Concluding unscientific postscripts*. Trans. David F. Swenson, Princeton, NJ: Princeton University Press.

Park, S. (2021). In defense of religious practicalism. *European Journal of Science and Theology*, 17(3), 27-38.

Park, S. (2016). *Great debates in philosophy*. South Korea: Korea Academic Information.

Plantinga, A. (1967/1990). *God and other minds: A study of the rational justification of belief in God*. Ithaca: Cornell University Press.

Rowe, W. (2007). *Philosophy of religion: An introduction*. Belmont, CA: Thomson Wadsworth.

12 CHAPTER

Ethics of Beliefs

1. Preamble

Is it (morally) right or wrong to believe something on faith? To put it differently, is it right or wrong to hold a belief on insufficient evidence? Two opposing answers to this question are defended by William Clifford (1845–1879) and William James (1842–1910). According to Clifford, under no circumstance is it right to believe something on faith. According to James, by contrast, under certain circumstances it is right to believe something on faith. We explore the debate between these two thinkers in this chapter.

2. Clifford

Clifford says, "It is wrong always, everywhere, and for anyone to believe anything on insufficient evidence" (Clifford, 1877, p. 460). Suppose that you are a shipowner. Your ship is old, so it might sink in the middle of an ocean. However, you believe that it will not sink. You have faith in your ship, so to speak. Your ship sails out with passengers on it to the ocean. It sinks in the mid-ocean, and all the passengers die. It was wrong for you to have faith in your ship. The deaths are due to your failure to proportion your belief to the evidence, i.e., due to your failure to determine the degree of your belief in accordance with the strength of evidence. To generalize, it is wrong to believe more than what evidence warrants.

Clifford thinks that even if your ship did not sink in the mid-ocean, it was wrong for you to believe that your ship would not sink. Why does Clifford think so? If we believe something on insufficient evidence, we "lose the habit of testing things and inquiring into them" (Clifford, 1877, p. 460). If we lose the habit, we would "sink back into savagery" (Clifford, 1877, p. 460). In other words, if we lose the critical mind, there would be no science and no civilization.

How would theists respond to Clifford's position that it is always wrong to believe something on insufficient evidence? They might appeal to illusory superiority (Hoorens, 1993). We tend to believe that we are more intelligent, drive better, look better than average. Such beliefs are useful in that they protect our self-esteem and mental health. Illusory superiority indicates that in some cases, it is morally permissible to form beliefs on insufficient evidence.

In light of such counterexamples, Clifford might give up his old position that under no circumstances is it right to believe something on insufficient evidence, and retreat to the modest position that *in most cases* it is wrong to believe something on insufficient evidence. Unlike the old position, the new position is immune to some examples in which it is right to believe something on insufficient evidence.

How would theists respond to Clifford's contention that if we believe something on insufficient evidence, we lose the habit of testing hypotheses and inquiring into things? They would point out that there are many scientists who believe in God. The scientists form religious beliefs on insufficient evidence, but they maintain the habit of testing hypotheses and inquiring into things. Therefore, it is questionable whether forming beliefs on insufficient evidence weakens our habit of testing hypotheses and inquiring into things.

3. James

James rejects Clifford's view that "It is wrong always, everywhere, and for anyone to believe anything on insufficient evidence" (Clifford, 1877, p. 460). On his account, it is right to believe something on faith, provided that "*where faith in a fact can help create the fact*" (James, 1984, p. 20). To state it otherwise, it is right to believe something on faith, provided that the belief of a fact contributes to the creation of the fact.

James' view can be illustrated by the following examples. Suppose that I do not have sufficient evidence for the belief that you like me, but I believe on faith that you like me. As a result of this belief, I treat you nicely and kindly, and you come to like me. Note that my unjustified belief that you like me contributes to the creation of the fact that you like me. In this case, it was right for me to believe on faith that you liked me.

As another example, suppose that you are a young scientist. You believe on faith that you can publish papers in Science, Nature, or Cell. As a result of this belief, you work hard, and you succeed in publishing papers in those journals. Note that your unjustified belief that you can publish papers in the journals contributes to the creation of the fact that you publish papers in the journals. In this case, it was right for you to believe on faith that you could publish papers in the journals.

Similarly, suppose that you believe on faith that God loves you. Your belief contributes to the creation of the fact that he loves you, i.e., he loves you in part as a result of your unjustified belief that he loves you. In this case, it was right for you to believe on faith that he loves you. Similar justifications can be given of other religious beliefs, such as the belief that he told us to love our neighbors.

What are we to make of James's defense of religious beliefs? Happiness might result from my belief that you like me, from my belief that I can publish papers in the top journals, and from my belief that God loves me. However, unhappiness might also result from those beliefs. For example, I might become arrogant as a result of my belief that he loves me. To go further, I might kill heretics as a result of my religious belief that he wants me to kill them. In such a case, it is questionable whether it was right for me to believe on faith that he loves me, or that he wants me to kill heretics.

Suppose that Christians, Muslims, and Hinduists claim that it right to believe on faith that God, Allah, and Vishnu exist, respectively, because beliefs in God, Allah, and Vishnu, help create the facts that God, Allah, and Vishnu exist. By contrast, atheists claim that it is right to disbelieve on maith that God, Allah, and Vishnu exist because disbeliefs in God, Allah, and Vishnu help create the facts that they do not exist. Who are right, Christians, Muslims, Hinduists, or atheists? James owes us an answer to this daunting question.

What if AI claims that it is right for it to believe on faith that God exists? Does AI's belief in him help create the fact that he exists? Does Neanderthals' belief in him help create the fact that he exists? It is not clear how James would answer this question. If he says "Yes," he would face the objection that it is degrading to God that a machine's thinking helps create the fact that he exists. If James says "No," he would have to explain why he thinks that a human' belief helps create the fact that God exists, but AI's belief does not.

Finally, what if I believe on insufficient evidence that you will get into a traffic accident, and that as a result you get into a traffic accident? In this case, my belief of a fact helped create the fact. Was it right or wrong for me to believe on insufficient evidence that you will get into a traffic accident? James owes us an answer to this question.

4. Summary

Clifford claims that under no circumstances is it right to believe something on insufficient evidence because we lose the habit of testing hypotheses and inquiring into things. However, it is questionable whether theists have the weaker habit of testing hypotheses and inquiring into things than atheists.

James claims that it is right to believe something on faith, provided that the belief of a fact helps create the fact. However, unhappiness might result from believing something on faith. Believers of different religions have faith in their own deities, and atheists might have maith in God. It is not clear whether AI's faith and Neanderthals' faith also help create religious facts.

Study Questions

1. Clifford claims that forming beliefs on insufficient evidence weakens our habit of testing hypotheses and inquiring into things, so it is morally wrong to believe on faith that God exists. How do you respond to him?

2. James claims that it is right to believe something on faith, provided that "*faith in a fact can help create the fact*" (James, 1984, p. 20). Provide an example to illustrate his claim. Do you accept or reject his claim? Why?

References

Clifford, W. (1877). The ethics of belief. In W. Rowe and W. Wainwright (Eds.),

Philosophy of religion: selected readings. Orlando, Florida: Harcourt Brace & Company.

Hoorens, V. (1993). Self-enhancement and superiority biases in social comparison. *European Review of Social Psychology*, 4(1), 113-139.

James, W. (1984). The will to believe. In J. Burr and M. Goldinger (Eds.), *Philosophy and contemporary issues*. New York: Macmillan.

CHAPTER 13

Life after Death & Pascal's Wager

1. Overview

Is there life after death? Should we believe in God to go to heaven after we die? In this chapter, we discuss five arguments for the existence of life after death and then Pascal's Wager, according to which we should believe in him to go to heaven after we die.

2. Life after Death

2.1. The Argument from Mediumship

Henry Price (1968) presents an interesting argument for the existence of life after death which might be called "the argument from mediumship." It holds that mediums can communicate with the deceased. A medium is a person who can allegedly be in touch with the dead. The medium can see the dead, and they can be *possessed* by them. The soul of a dead person allegedly gets into the medium's body, uses the medium's body, and talks through the medium's mouth.

Price recounts the case of Edgar Vandy. Edgar was drowned to death in 1933. His brother, George Vandy, consulted several mediums to investigate the cause of his brother's death. A medium said, "I get the letter H. He is wearing something belonging to your brother" (Price, 1968, p. 451). It was later discovered that Harold Vandy, Edgar's another brother, had worn Edgar's hat after Edgar died. The medium also stated that Edgar showed her a cigarette case and told her that it could be found in a particular place in

Edgar's house. In the place, George and the medium actually found an aluminum box which looked "exactly like a metal cigarette case" (Price, 1968, p. 451).

How did the medium know that someone whose name starts with "H" wore Edgar's hat? How did she know that an object looking like a cigarette case was in a particular place in Edgar's house? One possible hypothesis is that Edgar's soul existed and gave the information to the medium. Another possible hypothesis is that the medium was capable of ESP (Extra-Sensory Perception). ESP enabled the medium to see Harold Vandy wear Edgar's hat and the aluminum box located in a particular place in the house. If the first hypothesis is true, we can conclude that there is life after death. By contrast, if the second hypothesis is true, we cannot. Price wraps up his paper with the following advice to his readers: "Do not be too sure that you will not continue to exist as a person after your physical organism has died" (Price, 1968, p. 459). In other words, there might be life after death.

2.2. The Argument from Conformal Cyclic Cosmology

According to the Big Bang theory, the universe was an infinitely small point called "the singularity" about 13.8 billion years ago, and the singularity expanded at incredibly high speed. There was nothing before the Big Bang. There was neither space nor time. The universe has been expanding ever since the Big Bang, and it expands faster and faster.

Roger Penrose (2012) proposes an alternative to the Big Bang theory called "conformal cyclic cosmology." According to this cosmological model, the universe infinitely repeats the cycle of expansion and contraction. The universe is expanding now, but it will stop expanding, shrink ultimately to an infinitely small point, and then expand again. There were and will be infinitely many Big Bangs, and thus the universe has neither a beginning nor an end.

If conformal cyclic cosmology is true, it is *possible* that the universe reiterates the same physical processes, as it reiterates the cycle of expansion and contraction. It follows that I might have existed billions of years ago before the Big Bang, although I did not exist after I died billions of years ago. In addition, after I die several decades later, I might exist again billions of years later after the next Big Bang. Thus, I might be in the infinite cycle of short existence and long nonexistence.

23. The Argument from Near Death Experience

Some people allege that they have been to the world of the dead. They commonly have the experience of going through a long tunnel. They see a bright light at the end of the tunnel. They feel an extreme joy and see their deceased family members and friends. This kind of experience is called NDE (near death experience). NDE seems to show that the world of the dead exists.

However, neuroscientists discovered that a large amount of

endorphin is secreted in the brain of a person who has NDE. Consequently, there can be two hypotheses explaining why NDE occurs. The first hypothesis is that the world of the dead is the cause of NDE. The second hypothesis is that the endorphin is the cause of NDE. If we accept the second hypothesis, we do not need to accept the first hypothesis. Therefore, NDE does not establish the existence of the world of the dead.

Believers of the world of the dead would point out that the two hypotheses are compatible with each other, and they would embrace both hypotheses simultaneously, i.e., they would believe that NDE occurs because a large amount of endorphin is released in the brain and because the world of the dead exists. They might add that the world of the dead causes the brain to release endorphin.

In response, skeptics of the world of the dead would invoke Ockham's razor, according to which a simple hypothesis is better than a complex one, saying that we do not need to postulate the existence of the world of the dead, and we only need to postulate the existence of the endorphin to explain why NDE occurs. They might add that the endorphin is released in the brain due to the dying person's bodily conditions.

2.4. The Argument from God

In the previous subsections, we critically evaluated the three arguments for the existence of life after death. Theists might admit that all of them are weak. However, they would not give up their belief that life exists after death. How would they justify their belief? They would construct the argument that since God exists, life after death exists. On their account, he would ensure that life exists after death so that he could reward those who deserve reward and punish those who deserve punishment.

This new argument for the existence of life after death relies on the assumption that God exists. How can theists justify the assumption? They have no choice but to appeal to the traditional arguments for the existence of him, such as the arguments from design, miracles, religious experiences. As we have seen in the previous chapters, however, those arguments are vulnerable to various objections. Moreover, the problems of divine location, divine age, divine foreknowledge, and evil indicate that he does not exist.

In response, theists might construct a new argument for the existence of God that might be called "the argument from the Bible" according to which he exists because the Bible says so. The Bible is the perfect book, given that it is a collection of words from him, the perfect being. Everything that the Bible says is true.

Atheists would object that in addition to the Bible, there are other scriptures, such as the Quran and the Vedas. Which scripture should we choose? Moreover, there are unbelievable verses in scriptures. For example, the Bible says that heretics "must be destroyed" (Exodus 22:20). The Quran says that you should kill disbelievers "wherever you find them" (2:191). Therefore, just because the Bible says that God exists, it does not follow that he exists. Similarly, just because the Quran says that Allah exists, it does not follow that Allah exists.

25. The Argument from Panpsychism

Panpsychism is "the view that mentality is fundamental and ubiquitous in the natural world" (Goff et al., 2022). To say that mentality is fundamental means that the mind is not reducible to anything else, and that it is distinct from other fundamental features of reality, such as particles, waves, and fields. To say that it is ubiquitous means that it exists everywhere. At present, there is no empirical evidence for panpsychism, and thus it is merely a speculative assumption.

Panpsychists might speculate that just as an apple is composed of atoms, so the mind is composed of particles, that could be called "mental particles." Mental particles are distinct from atoms, but similar to them in that they are dispersed throughout the world, can neither be generated nor be destroyed, and are eternal. It might be that before a person is born, her mental particles are scattered around the world, but that after her brain is formed in her mother's womb, they become concentrated in it, and that after she dies, they will be dispersed again throughout the world.

According to quantum field theory, an apple is composed of fields, such as quark fields, the photon field, and the gluon field. A field is a fluid-like substance that permeates all of spacetime. It consists of points, each of which has a value that changes over time. Panpsychists might speculate that the mind is itself a field that could be called "the mental field." It is distinct from physical fields, but similar to them in that it is extends throughout spacetime, in that each of its points has a value that varies with time, and in that it is eternal. It might be that before a person is born, all the points of her mental field are slightly excited, but that after her brain is formed in her mother's womb, the points of her mental field in it are highly excited while other points of her mental field remain slightly excited, and that after she dies, all the points of her mental field will be slightly excited again.

An implication of panpsychism is that just as atoms and fields are eternal, so mental particles and the mental fields are eternal. At present, scientists do not formulate and test hypotheses about mental particles and mental fields. In the future, however, they might. Such hypotheses could reveal what properties they have and how they relate to physical particles and fields. Scientists might even invent scientific instruments capable of detecting them.

3. Pascal's Wager

Blaise Pascal (2018) claims that if God exists and you believe in him, you will go to heaven where you will enjoy his blessing forever. If he exists but you do not believe in him, you will go to hell where you will suffer from his damnation for good. What if he does not exist but you believe in him? You lose a little, such as having to go to church and follow his rules. What if he does not exist and you do not believe in him? You again a little, such as living life as you please. Therefore, you should believe in him.

In Chapter 1, we distinguished between true and useful beliefs. A true belief is one that corresponds to the world, whereas a useful belief is one that brings about happiness. We also noted that true beliefs might be useless, and useful beliefs might be false. Pascal's Wager asserts that we do not know whether the belief of God is true or false, but the belief of him might be useful. Therefore, we should believe in him.

Atheists might object that the probability that God exists is almost zero, given that there are no solutions to the problems of divine location, divine age, divine foreknowledge, and evil. To believe that he exists in spite of these problems is just as unreasonable as to buy a lottery ticket when the probability of winning the lottery is almost zero.

Pascalians, those who defend Pascal's Wager, would reply that if you go to heaven, you will be happy *for good*, which implies that the amount of happiness that the belief of God might bring about is infinite. Moreover, if you go to hell, you will be unhappy *forever*, which means that the amount of unhappiness that the disbelief of him might bring about is infinite. It follows that as long as the probability that he exists is not zero, it is reasonable to believe that he exists.

Critics of Pascal's Wager object that there is no sufficient evidence for belief in God, so it is psychologically impossible to believe in him. Pascal rejoins that you will acquire the belief of him, if you habitually perform religious rituals for a long time. In other words, you will end up believing in him unbeknownst to you, if you pray to him and sing religious songs together with other believers for a long time.

Pascal's Wager is at variance with St. Augustin's response to the problem of evil that we discussed in Chapter 9. St. Augustine suggests that evil exists due to human free will, and that God only respects human free will. Going along with St. Augustin's suggestion, atheists might argue that after we die, we will have the free will to go to heaven, and that he will only respect the free will. Accordingly, we do not need to believe in him before we die, and we only need to have the free will to go to heaven after we die.

St. Augustine might reply that God respects living persons' free will, but not souls' free will, and thus that disbelievers' souls, even if they have the free will to go to heaven, will go to hell. In response, atheists would argue that this possible reply is *ad hoc*, i.e., it calls for justification. Why is it that he respects living persons' free will, but not souls' free will? As it stands, it appears to be a discrimination against souls for him to respect living persons' free will, but not souls' free will. He should treat living persons and souls equally.

According to Pascal's Wager, God sends believers and nonbelievers to heaven and hell, respectively. This view on him does not go hand in hand with the teaching of Christianity that we should love even our enemies. Only broad-minded people can love their enemies, so Christianity teaches us to be broad-minded. However, he is narrow-minded in that he sends only believers to heaven. If he were broad-minded, he would also send nonbelievers to heaven. Nonbelievers, who are sent to heaven, would be moved and would start believing in him.

Finally, Pascal's Wager conflicts with the view that God is omniscient. He knew, even before you were born, whether you would go to heaven or hell. You do not know whether you will go to heaven or hell, but he does. The following dilemma can be constructed against Pascalians. On the one hand, if he knows that you will go to heaven, it is 100% probable that you will go to heaven. You will go to heaven even if you disbelieve in him, and hence it is only a waste of time to believe in him. On the other hand, if he knows that you will go to hell, it is 100% probable that you will go to hell. You will go to hell even if you believe in him, and hence it is only a waste of time to believe in him. Therefore, it does not matter whether he knows that you will go to heaven, or that you will go to hell. It is only a waste of time to believe in him. This dilemma is merely an application of Eleonore Stump's insight that we discussed in Chapter 2. According to her, if he is omniscient, it is difficult to "conceive of a satisfactory justification for petitionary prayer" (Stump, 1979, p. 81).

4. Summary

We discussed five arguments for the existence of life after death. The argument from mediumship holds that a medium can communicate with the dead, and thus there is life after death. The argument from conformal cyclic cosmology holds that the universe infinitely reiterates expansion and contraction, and thus there will be another life billions of years later after this life. The argument from near death experience holds that some people have the similar experience of seeing their deceased family members and friends, and thus the world of the dead exists. The argument from God holds that since he exists, life after death exists. The argument from panpsychism holds that the components of the mind are eternal.

Pascal's Wager holds that we should believe in God because to believe in him is the best bet. It is useful to believe in him, although it is not probable that he exists, because we might be rewarded with eternal happiness or punished with eternal unhappiness. However, Pascal's Wager is at variance with St. Augustine's free will defense against the problem of evil, with the view that he is broad-minded, and with the view that he is omniscient.

Study Questions

1. State and assess the five arguments for the existence of life after death. Do they show that we should believe in God to go to heaven?

2. Explicate Pascal's Wager. Do you accept or reject Pascal's Wager? Would God respect your free will to go to heaven? If not, why not? Is it broad–minded or narrow–minded for him to send only believers to heaven?

References

Goff, P., Seager, W., and Allen-Hermanson, S. (2022). Panpsychism. In E. Zalta (Ed.), *The Stanford encyclopedia of philosophy*. URL = 〈https://plato.stanford.edu/archives/sum2022/entries/panpsychism/〉.

Pascal, B. (2018). Pensée. Trans. W. Trotter. Mineola, New York: Dover Publications.

Penrose, R. (2012). *Cycles of time: An extraordinary new view of the universe*. New York: Random House.

Price, H. (1968). The problem of life after death. *Religious Studies*, 3(2), 447-459.

Stump, E. (1979). Petitionary prayer. *American Philosophical Quarterly*, 16(2), 81-91.

CHAPTER

14

The Problem of Divine Evaluation

1. Preamble

According to Pascal's Wager, God will evaluate us after we die, i.e., he will send us either to heaven or to hell depending on whether we believed in him while we were in this world. According to the Bible and the Quran, God and Allah will punish nonbelievers. The Bible states, for example, "But the cowardly, the unbelieving, the vile, the murderers, the sexually immoral, those who practice magic arts, the idolaters and all liars—they will be consigned to the fiery lake of burning sulfur. This is the second death" (Revelation 21:8). The Quran states, for example, "Allah has promised the hypocrites, men and women, and the disbelievers the Fire of Hell, therein shall they abide" (9:68) Is it right or wrong for God (and Allah) to punish disbelievers? Is God's evaluation system flawless or flawed? In this chapter, I argue that it is flawed, presenting several reasons for thinking so.

2. Objections to the Divine Evaluation

We have many human rights. One of them is the right to free thought. It is also known as the freedom of conscience. The idea is that we can think whatever we want to think, and yet we are not liable to the punishment from the government. The government cannot punish us on the ground that we have or do not have a certain thought. If the government punishes us on that ground, it violates the right to free thought. Only the government which is afraid of rebellion suppresses the right to free thought. God is omnipotent, so he must not be afraid of humans' rebellion against him. Sending nonbelievers to hell amounts to punishing them for not having a certain thought. It is not clear why he violates the human right to free thought (Park, 2024, p. 37).

In addition, it is questionable whether it is praiseworthy to believe in God, and whether it is blameworthy to disbelieve in him. If it is praiseworthy to believe in him, it must be similar to other praiseworthy actions, such as paying taxes and blood donation. If it is blameworthy to disbelieve in him, it must be similar to other blameworthy actions, such as evading taxes and stealing from others. It is not clear, however, what the similarities are between paying taxes and believing in him, and between evading taxes and disbelieving in him (Park, 2024, p. 38).

Theists might suggest that there are similarities between believing in God and paying taxes, and between disbelieving in him and evading taxes. Just as it maximizes happiness to pay taxes, so it maximizes happiness to believe in him. If you believe in him, both you and him will be happy. By contrast, just as it maximizes unhappiness to evade taxes, so it maximizes unhappiness to disbelieve in him. If you disbelieve in him, both you and he will be unhappy.

This reply prompts the following objections. God is omnipotent, so he does not need our beliefs of him in order to be happy, i.e., he can be happy even if we do not believe in him. In addition, he is broad-minded, so he would not be unhappy just because we disbelieve in him. It is a manifestation of human arrogance to say that he is happy or unhappy depending on whether we believe in him.

We might set aside the foregoing objections and grant that it is praiseworthy to believe in God and blameworthy to disbelieve in him. It is still disputable whether it is just or unjust for him to send believers to heaven and disbelievers to hell. To be sent to heaven means to be happy *forever*, and to be sent to hell means to be unhappy *forever*. Thus, to send believers to heaven amounts to rewarding them with an infinite amount of happiness, and to send disbelievers to hell amounts to punishing them with an infinite amount of unhappiness. The reward and the punishment are excessive (Park, 2024, pp. 39-40).

In general, the degrees of reward and punishment should be commensurate with the magnitude of praiseworthiness and blameworthiness of deeds. Suppose that you give a dollar to a beggar on the street, and that the government rewards you with one million dollars. Admittedly, your deed is commendable. However, the government's reward is excessive. Suppose also that you steal a dollar from others, and that the government punishes you with life imprisonment. Admittedly, your deed is reprehensible, but the government's punishment is excessive. The same goes for rewarding believers with eternal happiness and for punishing nonbelievers with eternal unhappiness. Rewarding believers with eternal happiness is excessive. So is punishing disbelievers with eternal unhappiness. A just evaluation system would issue the reward and the punishment of the right degrees to evaluatees. (Park, 2024, p. 40)

Let me turn to a different problem with God's evaluation system. Imagine that a professor issues only two grades to her students, viz., A and F. She does not assign other grades: B, C, and D. She evaluates her students' performances on the midterm exam and the final exam on the numerical scale. So she assigns to her students numerical scores, such as 56, 68, 78, etc. In the end, however, she draws a line at 70. Every student whose score is above 70 receives an A, and every student whose score is below 70 receives an F. How would students react to the professor's evaluation system? Students, especially those whose scores are right below 70, would be upset, thinking that the professor's evaluation system is unjust and unfair. A just and fair evaluation system should be more fine-grained than the professor's one, i.e., it should have other grades as well as As and Fs. The same goes for the divine evaluation system in which God issues only the two extreme grades: sending to heaven and hell.

Why should God's evaluation system include other grades? The belief of him comes in diverse lengths and degrees. One may believe in him for a year, ten years, or one hundred years. In addition, the degree of her belief of him may be 70%, 80%, 90%, or 100%. To believe in him with 100% degree means that she does not doubt at all that he exists. Now, how long and strongly should we believe in him to go to heaven? Imagine that you believed in him for 9.9 years, but he sends you to hell on the ground that he drew the line at 10 years. Or imagine that you believed in him with 89% degree, but he sends you to hell on the ground that he drew the line at 90%. You would be upset, thinking that his evaluation system is flawed (Park, 2024, p. 41).

Theists claim that you should not only believe that God exists but also live a religious life to go to heaven. But exactly what does "a religious life" mean? Suppose that you believe in him, but you miss church one time. Are you destined to go to heaven? Theists would say, "Yes." However, another question arises. What if you miss church two times? How about three times? Where does he draw the line? Why? Absent answers to this question, we can conclude that the divine evaluation system is vague, i.e., that it is not clear exactly what we should do to go to heaven, and hence who will go to heaven and who will go to hell. An evaluation system that produces an unpredictable outcome is imperfect. The more unpredictable its outcomes are, the worse the evaluation system is (Park, 2024, p. 47).

How about chimpanzees and AIs? Do they also go to heaven or hell depending on whether they believed in God? How about Neanderthals? Molecular biologists claim that there is only 1% genetic difference between chimpanzees and humans. Imagine that genetic mutations occur to chimpanzees in the future, and as a result there will be only 0.5% genetic difference between humans and chimpanzees? Will chimpanzees also go to heaven or hell depending on whether they believed in God? Absent answers to these questions, we can conclude that the divine evaluation system is vague. An evaluation system which is vague about its targets is imperfect (Park, 2024, p. 44).

How would theists reply to the foregoing objections to the divine evaluation system? They would argue that God is omniscient, that he knows who deserves to go to heaven and who deserves to go to hell, and that he knows exactly who and what the targets of his evaluation system are. Moreover, his evaluation system is perfect, and he enforces it fairly to all of his evaluatees. Unfortunately, it is unknown to us. (Park, 2024, p. 42)

We can ask the following questions about the alleged perfect evaluation system. Does it draw a line or not in the different lengths of belief, in the different degrees of belief, and in the different times of missing church? This question is important because it is problematic to draw a line and also problematic not to draw a line. It is problematic to draw a line because those who are right below a line will be sent to hell. It is problematic not to draw a line because an evaluatee has to be sent either to heaven or hell. This dilemma makes it clear that there is no perfect way for God to send evaluatees to heaven or hell.

We can set aside this dilemma and grant that God's evaluation system is perfect. It is still disputable whether it is morally right for him to act on the evaluation system without first opening it to his evaluatees. For now, it is not transparent to his evaluatees. Hence, we do not know exactly for how long and how strongly we should believe in him. Nor do we know exactly how many times we can and cannot miss church. An omnibenevolent and omnipotent being would make his perfect evaluation system public to his evaluatees before he enforces it on them (Park, 2024, p. 43).

All the objections that I raised above to the divine evaluation system leads to a philosophical problem that I call "the problem of divine evaluation" (Park, 2024, p. 48). It holds that the divine evaluation system is not perfect, and that it is doubtful that God, the perfect evaluator, exists. Those who believe that believers are sent to heaven and disbelievers are sent to hell have the burden of solving the problem of divine evaluation.

3. An Objection and a Reply

Theists would object that if we challenge God's evaluation system, we will be punished by him, and we will go to hell. Consequently, we should not criticize his evaluation system. Even if his evaluation system has flaws, we should accept it, worship him, and go to heaven under his evaluation system. In short, we should do our best to go to heaven instead of complaining about his evaluation system.

This objection paints God as if he does not tolerate criticisms against his policy, as if he is not interested in persuading his evaluatees that his evaluation system is fair, and as if he is narrow-minded and not omnibenevolent. He might be a deity. However, he does not count as God who is allegedly omnipotent, omniscient, and omnibenevolent. It is questionable whether such a deity deserves our worship.

4. Summary

God is alleged to be omnipotent and omnibenevolent. An omnibenevolent being would justly and fairly evaluate his evaluatees, i.e., he would issue the reward and the punishment of the right degrees to his evaluatees. His evaluation system, however, is unjust and unfair in multiple respects. It is a mystery why an omnipotent and omnibenevolent being designed and executes the flawed evaluation system on his evaluatees. Like the problem of evil, the problem of divine evaluation shows that the alleged perfect being does not exist.

Study Questions

1. Respond to at least one of the following objections to God's evaluation system. (i) He violates the human right to free thought. (ii) It is questionable whether it is praiseworthy to believe in him, and whether it is blameworthy not to believe in him. (iii) He excessively

rewards believers and excessively punishes nonbelievers. How would you improve his evaluation system? If you were him, how would you evaluate your evaluatees?

2. Respond to at least one of the following objections to God's evaluation system. (iv) He assigns to his evaluatees only the two extreme grades: sending to heaven and hell. (v) Pascal's Wager is silent on the issue of how long and how strongly we should believe in him to go to heaven. (vi) Pascal's Wager is silent on the issue of whether he evaluates chimpanzees and AIs. How would you improve his evaluation system? If you were him, how would you evaluate your evaluatees?

Reference

Park, S. (2024). The problem of divine evaluation. *Symposion*, 11(1), 37–48.

CHAPTER 15

The Problems of Heaven-Dwellers and Hell-Dwellers

1. Introduction

In this chapter, I explicate what I call "the problem of heaven-dwellers" and "the problem of hell-dwellers," and then explore theists' four possible attempts to solve them (Park, 2025). These problems are intended to show that the putative perfect being's evaluation system is not perfect, and thus that the alleged perfect being does not exist.

2. Problems

What is the problem of heaven-dwellers? Imagine that you believed in God while you were in this world, and thus that you are sent to heaven after you died. After you enjoy happiness in heaven for a while, you become arrogant and start disbelieving in him. What should he do to you? Should he send you to hell? This question creates the problem of heaven-dwellers.

What is the problem of hell-dwellers? Imagine that you disbelieved in God while you were in this world, and thus that you are sent to hell after you died. After you suffer in hell for a while, you repent that you disbelieved in him in this world, ask him to forgive you, and start believing in him. What should he do to you? Should he send you to heaven? This question creates the problem of hell-dwellers.

In the following section, I sketch four possible theist responses to the problems of heaven-dwellers and hell-dwellers, and then critically evaluate them.

3. Theists' Four Possible Responses

3.1. No Choice but to Believe

Theists might suggest that heaven-dwellers see God, that he tells them that he is God, and that he performs some miracles to convince them that he is God. In addition, whenever they see him, they feel high and experience euphoria. As a result, they cannot but believe in him, i.e., it is psychologically impossible for them to disbelieve in him.

This response to the problem of heaven-dwellers has the following four problems. (i) Heaven-dwellers might think to themselves that they are hallucinating or dreaming when they see God. As a result, they can be skeptical that they see him. (ii) They might disbelieve in him by the leap of maith, the opposite of faith. They see him, but they blindly disbelieve in him on maith. This idea oppositely echoes Aquinas's idea that we can believe in God on faith (Rowe, 2007, p. 93). (iii) Heaven-dwellers might regularly perform anti-religious rituals collectively to disbelieve in him, and as a result, they might end up disbelieving in him. This idea oppositely mirrors Pascal's advice: you might disbelieve in him, but if you go to church every Sunday and perform religious rituals for a long time, you will end up believing in him.

How about hell-dwellers? Theists might suggest that hell-dwellers do not see God, and thus they would not believe that he exists. Opponents would object that even if hell-dwellers cannot see him, they can believe in him on faith, or they might regularly perform religious rituals for a long time, and as a result they might end up believing in him.

3.2. Virtuous and Vicious Characters

Theists might suggest that heaven-dwellers are so virtuous that they always feel inclined to believe in God and never feel inclined to disbelieve in him. Timothy Pawl and Keven Timpe suggest that "In heaven, the blessed will be incapable of willing any sin, just as we are incapable of willing the particular sin of torturing an innocent child for a nickel, and just as Teresa is incapable of willing to swindle from a homeless shelter for a luxurious vacation" (Pawl and Timpe, 2009, p. 408). Mother Teresa is so virtuous that she always feels inclined to help the underprivileged and never feels inclined to take advantage of them. Her psychological structure does not allow her to use them. Similarly, heaven-dwellers' psychological structure does not allow them to disbelieve in God.

This suggestion gives rise to the suspicion that heaven-dwellers do not have the free will to choose between the belief and the disbelief of God, i.e., that heaven-dwellers are psychologically programmed to believe that he exists. If this suspicion is true, they are not free agents capable of choosing between the belief and the disbelief of him, but merely believing machines incapable of choosing between the belief and the disbelief of him.

How about hell-dwellers? Pawl and Timpe might also suggest that hell-dwellers' psychological structure does not allow them to believe in God. In my view, however, this suggestion gives rise to the suspicion that hell-dwellers do not have the free will to choose between the belief and the disbelief of him, i.e., that hell-dwellers are psychologically programmed to disbelieve that he exists. If this suspicion is true, they are not free agents but merely disbelieving machines.

In response, Pawl and Time suggest that heaven-dwellers have the free will to choose between competing good deeds, although they do not have the free will to choose between good and bad deeds. For example, they have "the choice either to sing in the heavenly choir or to play the harp" (Pawl and Timpe, 2009, p. 408). However, they do not have the free will to choose between good and bad deeds. Thus, they always do good things, and yet they have free will. The same goes mutatis mutandis for hell-dwellers. They have the free will choose between competing bad deeds, but they do not have the free will to choose between good and bad deeds.

What are we to make of Paul and Timpe's suggestion? It indicates that heaven-dwellers and hell-dwellers are merely robots programmed to do only good and bad things, respectively. Heaven-dwellers are programmed to do good things and to enjoy the reward from God, and hell-dwellers programmed to do bad things and to suffer the punishment from him. Heaven-dwellers are merely enjoying machines, and hell-dwellers are merely suffering machines.

It is not clear why God keeps rewarding the machines in heaven and keeps punishing the machines in hell. We usually reward our fellow humans so that they keep doing good things. We usually punish our fellow humans so that they refrain from doing bad things and so that they do good things. Heaven-dwellers, however, are so virtuous that they will keep doing good things even if God stops rewarding them. Hell-dwellers are so vicious that they will keep doing bad things even if he keeps punishing them. It is a mystery why he keeps rewarding good-behaving machines and punishing bad-behaving machines. What does he aim to achieve?

In addition, an omnipotent and omnibenevolent being would have switched the psychological structure of heaven-dwellers with that of humans. Specifically, he would have bestowed on humans the psychological structure which allows them only to believe in him, and he would have bestowed on heaven-dwellers the psychological structure which allows them both to believe and to disbelieve in him. If he switched the psychological structures this way, all of us would go to heaven and enjoy free will in heaven. It is a mystery why he created the psychological structures of humans and heaven-dwellers as he did.

33. Permanent Scores

Theists might suggest that heaven-dwellers and hell-dwellers have the free will to choose between the belief and the disbelief of God, that some heaven-dwellers disbelieve in him, and that some hell-dwellers believe in him. However, he does not send heaven-dwellers to hell and hell-dwellers to heaven. His policy states that once you are sent to heaven, you will stay in heaven forever, no matter what you do in heaven, and that once you are sent to hell, you will stay in hell forever, no matter what you do in hell.

On this account, life in this world is like a test. Once the test is over, God assigns a score to you, and you cannot change the score. Just as a professor does not reduce your score on the ground that you forgot your answer to a question after the exam, so God does not send heaven-dwellers to hell on the ground that they disbelieve in him. Just as a professor does not raise your score on the ground that you figured out the answer to a question after the exam, so God does not send hell-dwellers to heaven on the ground that they believe in him.

Consider, however, that God is omnibenevolent, which implies that he is just, and that a just being would treat his evaluatees in accordance with their deserts, i.e., he would reward those who deserve reward, and punish those who deserve punishment. Heaven-dwellers deserve punishment once they disbelieve in him, and hell-dwellers deserve reward once they believe in him. Therefore, heaven-dwellers should be sent to hell, and hell-dwellers should be sent to heaven.

If you are not convinced yet of the foregoing objection, I invite you to imagine that you and I disbelieved and believed in God for about 100 years in this world, respectively. You are sent to hell on the ground that you disbelieved in him for about 100 years in this world. After you are sent to hell, you believe in him for a billion years, but he keeps you in hell. By contrast, I am sent to heaven on the ground that I believed in him for about 100 years in this world. After I am sent to heaven, I disbelieve in him for a billion years, but he keeps me in heaven. It is not fair for him to keep you in hell forever and keep me in heaven forever.

3.4. Reevaluations

Theists might now suggest that God regularly inspects heaven-dwellers and hell-dwellers, and sends heaven-dwellers to hell and hell-dwellers to heaven, depending on whether they believe in him. An immediate objection to this suggestion is that it is not clear exactly who are sent to heaven and who are sent to hell. Heaven-dwellers might disbelieve in him for 90 years, 80 years, and so on. Where does he draw the line? Why? The same question can be raised mutatis mutandis about hell-dwellers.

Theists might reply that God sends heaven-dwellers to hell the moment they disbelieve in him, and that he sends hell-dwellers to heaven the moment they believe in him. There are a couple of problems with this suggestion. (i) We would not be motivated to believe in him in this world, thinking that we only need to believe in him after we die. Moreover, it would be a good idea to spend some time in hell because a moderate amount of pain makes us mentally mature. As a result, we do not need to go to church while we are in this world. (ii) He does not send humans to heaven the moment they believe in him in this world, and that he does not send humans to hell the moment they disbelieve in him in this world. He waits until they die. Why does he treat humans differently from heaven-dwellers and hell-dwellers?

4. Summary

What should God do to heaven-dwellers who started disbelieving in him? Theists might offer the following answers. Heaven-dwellers see him, so they have no choice but to believe in him. Heaven-dwellers are so virtuous that they are psychologically inclined to believe in him. He does not send heaven-dwellers to hell. He regularly reevaluates heaven-dwellers and send disbelievers to hell. However, these answers are all vulnerable to objections. Similar answers and objections can be made vis-à-vis the issue of what he should do to hell-dwellers who started believing in him.

Study Questions

1. Evaluate theists' first and second responses to the problems of heaven–dwellers and hell–dwellers in Subsections 3.1 and 3.2. If you were a theist, how would you solve the problems of heaven–dwellers and hell–dwellers?

2. Assess theists' third and fourth responses to the problems of heaven–dwellers and hell–dwellers in Subsections 3.3. and 3.4. If you were a theist, how would you solve the problems of heaven–dwellers and hell–dwellers?

References

Park, S. (2025). The problems of disbelievers in heaven and believers in hell. *Symposion*, 12 (1), 43–54.

Pawl, T. and Timpe, K. (2009). Incompatibilism, sin, and free will in heaven. *Faith and Philosophy*, 26(4), 398–419.

Rowe, W. (2007). *Philosophy of religion: An introduction*. Belmont, CA: Thomson Wadsworth.

16

CHAPTER

Religious Language

1. Preamble

How should we interpret religious sentences? Consider the following verse in the Bible:

> In the beginning, God created the heavens and the earth. The earth was without form and void, and darkness was over the face of the deep. And the Spirit of God was hovering over the face of the waters. And God said, 'Let there be light,' and there was light. (Genesis 1:1–3)

Are these sentences meaningful or meaningless? Are they descriptions of reality or expressions of emotions? Are they capable of being true or false? Philosophers of different schools of thought have opposing answers to these questions. We go over them one by one in this chapter.

2. Logical Positivism

According to logical positivism (Ayer, 1936), a sentence is meaningful if and only if it is empirically verifiable, i.e., if and only if we can get observational evidence that would prove that it is true. Consider the sentences, for example, "The sky is blue" and "The moon revolves around the earth." They are empirically verifiable. After all, we can have observational evidence for them. Consequently, they are meaningful, and they are either true or false. The same goes for other sentences in science, such as "There are black holes." By contrast, consider Heidegger's famous sentence "Nothing nothings." This sentence is not empirically verifiable, so it is meaningless, and it is neither true nor false. It is similar to a meaningless noise, "dkgicg."

Logical positivism implies that religious sentences are meaningless because they are not empirically verifiable. Consider religious sentences, such as "God created the world" and "God sends believers to heaven and nonbelievers to hell." We cannot get observational evidence that would prove that these sentences are true. It follows that they are meaningless, and that they are neither true nor false. They are similar to the meaningless noise "dkgicg." The former are not descriptions of reality any more than the latter is.

An immediate objection to logical positivism is that it is not clear how it can handle moral sentences, such as "Blood donation is right" and "Stealing is wrong." These sentences are meaningful. After all, we know what they mean. However, we cannot prove that they are true, given that we cannot observe the properties of rightness and wrongness in the world. For example, when you donate blood, we can see a needle on your arm and your blood flowing from your arm to the blood bag, but we cannot see the property of rightness in your action of donating blood (Hume, 1978, pp. 468-469). Therefore, logical positivism implies that moral sentences are meaningless, and that they are similar to the meaningless noise "dkgicg." However, our intuition says that they are meaningful. Therefore, logical positivism is false.

3. Emotivism

According to emotivism (Stevenson, 1944), a moral sentence is not a description of the world but rather an expression of emotion. Consider the sentence, "The moon revolves around the earth." It is a description of the world, so it is either true or false. By contrast, consider the sentences, "An apple, hurrah!" and "An orange, boo!" These sentences are not descriptions of an apple and an orange but rather expressions of tastes, so they are neither true nor false. The same goes for moral sentences. When I say, "Blood donation is right," I am expressing a positive emotion toward donating blood. When I say, "Stealing is wrong," I am expressing a negative emotion toward stealing. Since moral sentences are not descriptions of the world but rather expressions of emotion, they are neither true nor false.

There are similarities and differences between logical positivism and emotivism. A similarity between them is that both affirm that moral sentences are neither true nor false. A difference between them is that logical positivism asserts moral sentences are meaningless, whereas emotivism asserts that they are meaningful. On the emotivist account, moral sentences have emotive contents, but not factual contents.

Emotivists would suggest that a religious sentence is also an expression of emotion. Suppose that you have a job interview tomorrow, and that your friend says to you, "God will help you." On the emotivist account, your friend's sentence "God will help you" is not a description of what will happen tomorrow, i.e., it is not a prediction of a future event. It is rather an expression of her wish that you will pass the job interview. Accordingly, it is neither true nor false. When religious people say, "God created the world," their sentence is not a description of what happened in the past, but rather an expression of frustration regarding the origin of the world. Consequently, it is neither true nor false. When they say, "God sends believers and disbelievers to heaven and hell, respectively," they are not describing reality but rather they are expressing their wish that God sends believers and disbelievers to heaven and hell, respectively. Therefore, their sentence is neither true nor false.

In short, religious sentences do not have factual contents but emotive contents, and thus they are neither true nor false.

4. Religious Fictionalism

According to religious fictionalism (Scott, 2017), religious discourse is a fiction, which implies that religious entities, such as God, heaven, and hell, are all fictional ones like Superman and Batman. Superman and Batman do not exist, so sentences about them, such as "Superman can fly" and "Batman wears a black cloak," are all false. Similarly, religious entities do not exist, so religious sentences about them, such as "God created the world" and "God sends believers to heaven and nonbelievers to hell," are all false.

There are similarities and differences between emotivism and religious fictionalism. A similarity between them is that they both deny that religious entities are real, and that religious sentences are true. A difference between them is that emotivism asserts that religious sentences are expressions of emotions, whereas religious fictionalism asserts that they are descriptions of reality. On the emotivist account, religious sentences do not even purport to describe reality, whereas on the fictionalist account, they purport to describe reality, but they are all false.

5. Religious Skepticism

According to religious skepticism (Park, 2021), religious statements are true or false, but we do not have sufficient evidence to determine whether they are true or false. Consider religious sentences, such as "God created the world" and "God sends believers to heaven and nonbelievers to hell." They are descriptions of reality, so they are either true or false depending on whether they correspond to reality. However, we do not have enough evidence to determine whether they correspond to reality.

There are similarities and differences between religious fictionalism and religious skepticism. A similarity between them is that they both assert that religious sentences are descriptions of reality, so they are either true or false depending on whether they correspond to reality. A difference between them is that religious fictionalism rules out, while religious skepticism does not, the possibility that religious entities might exist, and that religious sentences might be true. In other words, religious fictionalism asserts that all religious statements are false, while religious skepticism asserts that they might be true or might be false.

Pascalians, those who advocate Pascal's Wager, would reject religious fictionalism and accept religious skepticism (Park, 2021). Religious fictionalism asserts that religious entities, such as God, heaven, and hell, do not exist, and thus that it is impossible for us to go to heaven or hell. By contrast, religious skepticism asserts that religious entities *might* exist, and that we might go to heaven or hell. Therefore, Pascal's Wager dovetails with religious skepticism, but clashes with religious fictionalism.

6. Religious Realism

According to religious realism, some religious entities, such as God, heaven, and hell are real, that some religious sentences are true, and that we have sufficient evidence for them. Consider religious sentences, such as "God created the world" and "God sends believers to heaven and nonbelievers to hell." They are descriptions of reality, so they are either true or false depending on whether they correspond to reality. In addition, we *know* that they are true. Thus, they are similar to some nonreligious sentences, such as "The sky is blue" and "The earth is round." Just as we know that the earth is round, so we know that God created the world, and that he sends believers to heaven and nonbelievers to hell.

Religious realism would be agreeable to believers and disagreeable to disbelievers. Believers think that traditional arguments, such as the argument from design and the argument from religious experiences, are strong enough to show that God is real. By contrast, disbelievers think that traditional arguments are not strong enough to show that he is real. Thus, believers and disbelievers would have different views on what counts as sufficient evidence.

7. Sufficient Evidence

The dispute between believers and disbelievers raises an interesting issue. How much evidence is sufficient? What is the definition of sufficient evidence? My brief answer to this question is "It depends." In some contexts, a small amount of evidence is regarded as sufficient. In other contexts, a large amount of evidence is regarded as insufficient. For example, prosecutors take a small amount of evidence to be sufficient when they consider whether to prosecute ordinary citizens, people who do not have power. By contrast, they take a large amount of evidence to be insufficient when they deliberate on whether to prosecute powerful people, such as themselves, judges, and lawmakers.

In general, the higher the stakes are, the more evidence is required to convince people. The stakes of religious issues are higher than the stakes of scientific issues. You should present a larger amount of evidence to persuade your religious opponents regarding religious issues than to persuade your scientific opponents regarding scientific issues. If the stakes are high enough, you will never be able to persuade your opponents no matter how much evidence you might present to your opponents. The stake is infinitely high when it comes to religious issues. In simple English, theists think that they will lose infinite happiness, if they stop believing in God. Consequently, atheists will never be able to persuade theists, no matter how much evidence they might present to theists.

8. Summary

According to logical positivism, religious sentences are meaningless because they are not empirically verifiable. According to emotivism, religious sentences are expressions of emotion. According to religious fictionalism, all religious sentences are false. According to religious skepticism, we do not have sufficient evidence to determine whether religious sentences are true or false. According to religious realism, we know that some religious sentences are true. How much evidence is sufficient? A small amount of evidence is regarded as sufficient in some contexts, while a large amount of evidence is regarded as insufficient in other contexts.

Study Questions

1. Apply logical positivism, emotivism, religious fictionalism, religious

skepticism, and religious realism to the religious sentences, "Jesus cured cancer patients," and "Jesus was resurrected." Which is the most reasonable interpretation of the religious sentences?

2. Koreans perform a sort of religious ritual on the Lunar New Year's Day. They put the ritual food on a ritual table and give two big bows to their ancestral tablets or to their ancestors' souls. Suppose that your father says, "Our ancestors' souls eat the food. If we serve them well, they will bring happiness and prosperity to us." Apply logical positivism, emotivism, religious fictionalism, religious skepticism, and religious realism to the religious sentences. Which is the most reasonable interpretation of the religious sentences?

References

Ayer, A. (1936). *Language, truth, and logic*. London: Victor Gollancz Ltd.

Hume, D. (1978). *A treatise of human nature*. L. A. Selby-Bigge and P. H. Nidditch (Eds.), Oxford: Oxford University Press.

Park, S. (2021). In defense of religious practicalism. *European Journal of Science and Theology*, 17(3), 27-38.

Scott, M. (2017). Religious language. In E. Zalta (Ed.), *The Stanford encyclopedia of philosophy*. URL = ⟨https://plato.stanford.edu/archives/win2017/entries/religious-language/⟩.

Stevenson, C. (1944). *Ethics and language*. New Haven: Yale University Press.

17 CHAPTER

The Conflicts between Science and Religion

1. Introduction

A perennial question in philosophy of religion is how religion relates to science. Some thinkers claim that they are compatible with each other, while other thinkers claim that they are incompatible with each other. This chapter explores a few conflicts between religion and science, and then possible theist responses to them.

2. Determinism vs. Free Will

Theists claim that we have freedom of choice. For example, St. Augustine claims that evil exists because we have free will, and thus that we should not blame God but ourselves for the existence of evil (Section 2 of Chapter 9). Some theists claim that we can choose to believe in him or to disbelieve in him, and thus that we should blame ourselves for going to hell after we die. If free will is an illusion, such religious doctrines are not tenable.

What does it mean to say that we have free will? It means that we have the ability to do otherwise. For example, we can choose between committing murder or not committing murder. Science tells us, however, that we do not have free will, and that we are like robots acting in accordance with laws of nature. Suppose, for example, that I throw a material object upwards, and that it falls down. The two events – throwing the material object upwards and its falling down – are necessarily connected with each other by the law of gravity. If the first event occurs, the second event *must* occur, i.e., the second event is *determined* to occur. Thus, successive events are necessarily connected with each other by a law of nature.

This view on the connection between successive events is called "determinism" in philosophy. It holds that events that occur were determined to occur by their prior conditions and laws of nature. An alternative formulation of determinism is that every event has a cause, and that if a cause occurs, an effect *must* occur, i.e., given the past, the present cannot be otherwise. For example, throwing a material object upwards is the cause, and its falling down is the effect. Given that it is thrown upwards, it must fall down, and it cannot be otherwise. All objects, including humans, obey laws of nature. Therefore, all human actions that occur were determined to occur by their prior conditions and laws of nature.

Determinism seems to be incompatible with free will. We may think that a murderer has chosen to commit murder. According to determinism, however, right before the murderer committed murder, there was a prior condition, and the murder was necessarily connected with the prior condition by a law of nature. The murderer was determined to commit murder due to the prior condition and the law of nature. The prior condition and the law of nature might be presently unknown to us, but they will be discovered in the distant future when we will have advanced science. The same goes for all the other human actions.

Let me use an analogy to cast light on determinism. Suppose

that trains have consciousness, but they are blind, so they cannot see railroads. As they run on railroads, they think that they change their directions as they wish. It is obvious to them that they run in particular directions because they want to run in those directions. As a result, they strongly believe that they have free will. Now, are trains right to think that they have free will? The answer is "No." Although it is obvious to them that they choose their directions, they are not choosing their directions. After all, the directions were fixed by railroads which they cannot see. They will see railroads, once they acquire powerful headlights. Similarly, we cannot see the factors that led murderers to commit murder, but we will see them, once we have advanced science in the future.

A scientific experiment seems to show that we do not have free will. There are one-to-one correlations between mental and brain states. For example, when we feel the desire to move our finger, a brain event occurs, and when the brain event occurs, we feel the desire to move our finger. Do the mental and brain events occur at the same time or at different times? According to Benjamin Libet's (1985) experiment, a brain event occurs, and 400ms later its corresponding mental event occurs. Thus, even before we feel the desire to move our finger, the brain event occurs, and a neural impulse travels to the finger. The finger moves as a result of the neural impulse. It appears that conscious decision does not contribute to the production of human actions. On the basis of Libet's experiment, Daniel Wegner (2017) concludes that we do not have free will.

The debate goes on in the literature between the advocates of free will and determinism over the issue of whether we have free will or not.

3. Religion vs. Evolutionary Theory

There is a conflict between creationism and evolutionary theory regarding the issue of speciation. Creationism asserts that species were created independently of each other, and that they are firmly fixed, i.e., that they do not become different species, and that a new species cannot branch off from an old species. According to evolutionary theory, however, all current organisms on the earth stemmed from the common ancestor, single-celled organisms, which implies that a species can become a different species, i.e., that a new species can branch off from an old species.

There is a conflict between religion and evolutionary theory regarding the issue of a hierarchy of beings. Dante (1265-1321) claims that there is a hierarchy of beings. God is at the top, angels are below him, humans are below angels, and nonhuman animals are at the bottom. According to evolutionary theory, however, all current organisms on the earth originated from single-celled organisms, which implies that humans and nonhuman animals are on a par, i.e., that nonhuman animals are our cousins.

There is a conflict between religion and evolutionary theory regarding the origin of morality. Theists claim that God is the origin of morality. He gave us the Ten Commandments. Without him, there would be no moral rules, such as "Love your neighbors" and "Don't commit adultery." However, evolutionary theory asserts that we have moral rules because the behavioral tendency to observe moral rules was an adaptive trait.

This brief explanation can be fleshed out as follows. In the distant past, our ancestors did not observe moral rules. A variation occurred to them, i.e., some babies were born with the tendency to observe moral rules. The tendency was fitness-conducive, i.e., it increased their viability and fertility. After they grew up, they had their own babies. Their babies also had the tendency. As time passed, those with the tendency persisted, while those without the tendency perished. As a result, we have the tendency.

4. Different Realms

How would theists respond to the conflicts between science and religion? They might claim that science and religion belong to different realms, i.e., that science belongs to the realm of reason while religion belongs to the realm of faith. On the basis of this distinction between the two realms, they might conclude that religious believers can keep their religious beliefs although they conflict with science. For example, they can keep the belief that a species cannot become a different species although science claims that many new species emerged from old species.

Let me make three critical comments on this defense of religious beliefs. First, there is no strict distinction between science and religion. It is difficult to determine whether some beliefs are religious or scientific, e.g., "God triggered the Big Bang" and the belief "Love your neighbors." In addition, some religious beliefs are problematic, e.g., "Whoever sacrifices to any god other than the LORD must be destroyed" (Exodus 22:20). It is unreasonable to stick to such beliefs on the ground that science and religion belong to different realms.

Second, it is not clear whether science and religion belong to different realms. Some creationists claim that creationism is a scientific hypothesis, and it should be taught in school. On their account, creationism has a legitimate place in science education like scientific theories, such as the Big Bang theory. It is problematic for such creationists to suggest that science and religion belong to different realms, and thus that religious believers can maintain their religious beliefs although they conflict with science.

Third, we can construct the following reductio ad absurdum. Suppose that fortunetellers argue that science and fortunetelling belong to different realms, and thus that no matter what science says about fortunetelling, they can stick to their fortunetelling beliefs and to their business of making money from people who are worried about their future. Fortunetellers' position and believers' position are in the same boat.

Of course, religious believers would protest that religion is different from fortunetelling. However, they owe us an account of why it is that their position is defensible while fortunetellers' position is not. After all, fortunetellers would rather think that their position is defensible while religious believers' position is not. It is not clear how religious people can persuade fortunetellers that they are right and fortunetellers are wrong. Why is it that religious people can say that science and religion belong to different realms, so religious people can hang onto their religious beliefs even if their religious beliefs conflict with science, but that fortunetellers cannot say that science and fortunetelling belong to different realms, so fortunetellers hang onto their fortunetelling beliefs even if their fortunetelling beliefs conflict with science?

5. Summary

There are conflicts between science and religion. Creationism claims that a species is firmly fixed, and that human beings are above other organisms. By contrast, evolutionary theory claims that a species is not fixed, and that human beings are neither above nor below other organisms. Religious believers claim that we have free will. However, scientific research indicates that we do not have free will.

Religious believers might claim that science and religion belong to different realms, and thus that they can stick to their religious beliefs although their religious beliefs conflict with science. In response, nonbelievers would raise the following three objections.

(i) It is difficult to determine whether some beliefs are religious or scientific. (ii) Some creationists claim that creationism should be taught in a science classroom. (iii) Fortunetellers might say absurdly that fortunetelling and science belong to different realms, and thus that they can stick to their fortunetelling beliefs although their fortunetelling beliefs conflict with science.

Study Questions

1. Expound the conflict between free will and determinism. How do you respond to the conflict and to the suggestion that science and religion belong to different realms?

2. Explicate the conflict between creationism and evolutionary theory. How do you respond to the conflict and to the suggestion that science and religion belong to different realms?

References

Libet, B. (1985). Unconscious cerebral initiative and the role of conscious will in voluntary action. *The Behavioral and Brain Sciences*, 8(4), 529–566.

Wegner, D. (2017). *The illusion of conscious will*. Cambridge, Massachusetts: MIT Press.

18

CHAPTER

Evolutionary Theory

1. Preamble

Evolutionary theory is the paradigm for current biology, just as quantum mechanics and the theory of relativity are the paradigms for current physics. To say so implies that evolutionary theory is the most fundamental theory in current biology, just as quantum mechanics and the theory of relativity are the most fundamental theories in current physics. In this chapter, I lay out the structure of evolutionary theory and introduce evolutionary psychology. Evolutionary theory is useful in understanding religion, as will become clear in the remaining chapters of this book.

2. The Two Core Ideas

The two core ideas of evolutionary theory are the tree of life and the principle of natural selection (Sober, 2018, pp. 7–9). The tree of life is a description of the genealogical relations between past and current organisms. It makes the following noteworthy claims. Humans have not descended from monkeys but rather from hominids, and hominids are the common ancestor of both humans and monkeys. Hominids descended from fish, and fish have descended ultimately from single-celled organisms. The single-celled organisms are, the tree of life implies, the common ancestor of all living organisms on the earth today.

The tree of life also implies that new species emerged from old species. For example, humans evolved from hominids. Humans and hominids are different species. To say that two groups of organisms are different species means, roughly, that they cannot produce (fertile) offspring together. For example, a lion and a tigress belong to different species, although they can produce a liger together, because a liger cannot have offspring. Even if hominids and humans lived in the same period and in the same place, they could not have (fertile) children together. It follows that they are different species.

How did new species branch off from old species? What mechanisms were responsible for speciation? The main mechanism, according to evolutionary theory, is natural selection. Natural selection requires the following three conditions. (i) A variation must occur, i.e., some organisms must be born with a new property. (ii) The new property must be adaptive, i.e., it must increase the survivability and reproducibility of organisms. (iii) It must be heritable, i.e., it must be passed on to next generations. Once these three conditions are all met, natural selection occurs. In short, natural selection requires heritable variations in fitness (Sober, 2018, p. 9).

Natural selection is invoked to explain biological phenomena. For example, why do eagles have good eyesight? The evolutionary answer goes as follows. In the past, eagles did not have good eyesight. A variation occurred to them, i.e., some eaglets were born with good eyesight. They had a better chance to survive and reproduce than other eagles whose eyesight was as bad as that of their parents. Good eyesight made the former more likely to survive and reproduce than the latter. Good eyesight was passed on to next generations. As time passed, eagles with good eyesight persisted, while eagles with bad eyesight perished. As a result, current eagles have good eyesight.

Similar answers can be given to others questions: why do giraffes in Africa have long necks? Why do elephants in Africa have long noses? Why do snow leopards have long tails? Why do some butterflies have eyespots on their wings? I do not unfold answers to these questions because they can be extrapolated from the foregoing explanation of why eagles have good eyesight.

3. Evolutionary Psychology

Evolutionary theory can be used to explain not only physical properties, such as long necks and tails, but also mental properties, such as pain, hunger, love, fear, and joy. In evolutionary psychology, psychologists explain mental properties in terms of evolutionary theory. Let me provide the following four examples.

Parents love their children. Why do parents have this psychological property? In the distant past, our ancestors did not have the psychological propensity. A variation occurred to them, i.e., some babies were born with the psychological propensity to love their offspring. They grew up and had their own children. Their children had a better chance to survive and reproduce than their competitors who were born from parents who did not have the psychological property. The former also grew up and had their own children. Their children also had the psychological propensity. As time passed, those with the psychological propensity persisted, while those without the psychological propensity perished. As a result, current parents have the psychological propensity to love their children.

We feel repulsed by snakes. When we see snakes, we tend to step back. Why do we have this psychological feature? In the distant past, our ancestors did not feel repulsed by snakes. A variation occurred to them, i.e., some babies were born with the psychological feature. It was fitness-conducive, i.e., it increased the probability that they survived and reproduced. They grew up and had their own babies. Their babies also had the psychological feature. As time passed, the number of humans with the psychological tendency increased, while the number of humans without the psychological tendency decreased. As a result, most of us feel repulsed by snakes today.

We fear death. Why do we have this psychological trait? In the distant past, our ancestors did not fear death. A variation occurred to them, i.e., some babies were born with the psychological trait. The psychological trait was an adaptive one, i.e., it increased their survivability and reproducibility. They grew up and had their own offspring. Their children also had the psychological trait. As time passed, those with the psychological trait persisted, while those without the property perished. As a result, we fear death today.

We have the amazing mental ability to read other people's minds. When we look at a smiling face, for example, we can infer that our target agent is happy. When we look at a frowning face, we can infer that our target agent is unhappy. What enables us to accomplish these difficult tasks? Let me use an analogy to answer this question. If you insert a coin into a vending machine, you can get a cup of coffee from it. A vending machine is a system that takes a coin as an input, works on the input, and gives out a cup of coffee as an output. Cognitive psychologists hypothesize that the mind consists of many cognitive systems, one of which is theory of mind (ToM). ToM takes the perception of a facial expression as an input, works on it, and gives out the judgment that a target agent is in a certain mental state. Thus, it is ToM that enables us to attribute mental states to others.

What if ToM breaks down? In other words, what if ToM malfunctions? We suffer from a neurological disorder called "autism" (Baron-Cohen, Leslie, and Frith, 1985). Autistic people do not have the cognitive ability to read other people's minds. They have no idea what other people feel, believe, desire, and so forth. They cannot tell the difference between cognitive agents and inanimate objects, i.e., they do not know the difference between the objects that have minds and the objects that do not have minds. Thus, they treat human beings as if they are inanimate objects.

Why do we have ToM? Evolutionary psychology gives the

following answer. In the distant past, our ancestors did not have ToM. A variation occurred to them. Some babies were born with ToM. ToM was an adaptive trait. Our ancestors formed a society and lived together. Those with ToM knew whether others are happy or unhappy while those without ToM did not. The former had the better chance to survive and reproduce than the latter. The former grew up and had their own offspring. Their offspring also had ToM. As time passed, the number of the individuals with ToM increased, while the number of the individuals without ToM decreased. As a result, we have ToM today.

4. Goal

Evolutionary theory invokes past events to explain a current property, whether the current property is physical or mental. For example, evolutionary theory talks about what happened in the past to explain why current giraffes in Africa have long necks, and to explain why current parents love their children. It does not talk about the goal of an organism. It does not say, for example, that giraffes acquired long necks because they have the goal to eat the leaves on high branches, and that parents love their children because they have the goal to raise their children.

In this context, it is useful to distinguish between a teleological explanation and a mechanical explanation. A goal is invoked in a teleological explanation, while a cause is invoked in a mechanical explanation. It is a teleological explanation, for example, that a high school student applied for UNIST because he had the goal to win a Nobel prize. It is a mechanical explanation, for example, that a smoker got lung cancer because he smoked a pack of cigarette a day for twenty years. Aristotle thinks that both teleological and mechanical explanations are acceptable in science. By contrast, modern scientists, such as Newton and Darwin, think that only mechanical explanations are acceptable in science.

5. Summary

The tree of life and the principle of natural selection are at the heart of evolutionary theory. Natural selection requires heritable variations in fitness. Evolutionary theory explains not only physical properties but also mental properties. Evolutionary psychology applies evolutionary theory to diverse mental phenomena, including the fear of death and the ability to read others' minds. ToM is a cognitive system which enables us to attribute mental states to others. The malfunction of ToM leads to autism. Evolutionary explanation is not teleological but mechanical. A mechanical explanation is scientific while a teleological explanation is not.

Study Questions

1. Why do giraffes have long necks? Why do we fear death? Why do we

have ToM? Use evolutionary theory to answer these questions.

2. Distinguish between mechanical and teleological explanations. Be sure to provide examples. Provide an evolutionary explanation of why some butterflies have eyespots on their wings. Is the explanation mechanical or teleological? Is it legitimate to say that we live in order to achieve happiness, to worship God, or to please him?

References

Baron-Cohen, S., Leslie, A., and Frith, U. (1985). Does the autistic child have a "theory of mind"? *Cognition*, 21(1), 37-46.

Sober, E. (2018). *Philosophy of biology*. New York: Routledge.

CHAPTER 19

The Origin of Religion

1. Overview

What is the origin of religion? Why do some people hold religious beliefs? Where did religious beliefs come from? This chapter answers these questions from emotional, philosophical, neuroscientific, cognitive, and evolutionary perspectives. These perspectives cast light on the different aspects of the origin of religion.

One caveat is in order. The perspectives are not intended to refute religious beliefs. Even if the perspectives are all true, religious beliefs might be true. It is one thing to say that the former are true; it is another to say that the latter are false. An additional work is required to show that the latter are false.

2. The Five Hypotheses

2.1. The Emotional Hypothesis

The emotional hypothesis holds that some people believe in God because they are emotionally unstable. A study (Chen, 2010) suggests that people become more religious when the economy is bad. Another study (Bentzen, 2019) suggests that the number of religious people increases when an earthquake occurs. I add that people are more inclined to believe in God when they are seriously ill and when they are in a battlefield.

People do not turn to God when they are emotionally stable. Danes and Swedes "don't worship Jesus or Vishnu, don't revere sacred texts, don't pray, and don't give much credence to the essential dogmas of the world's great faiths" (Zuckerman, 2008, p. 2). In Denmark and Sweden, the crime rate is low, and government services are reliable. In addition, poverty and economic inequality are not found in those countries. This story of the two countries illustrates that people are less religious when they enjoy stable and predictable lives (Norris and Inglehart, 2004).

2.2. The Philosophical Hypothesis

The philosophical hypothesis holds that some people believe in God as a result of being convinced of the philosophical arguments for the existence of God that we discussed in earlier chapters of this book. They are the argument from design, the argument from miracles, the argument from religious experiences, and the ontological argument.

The philosophical hypothesis is problematic. The philosophical arguments for the existence of God are plagued by objections, as we noted in earlier chapters. As Blaise Pascal (2018) admits, they fail to show that God exists. Consequently, they cannot be the origin of belief in God and other religious beliefs.

In my view, some theists are psychologically predisposed to believe in God independently of the philosophical arguments. They fear death. As a result, they wish that he existed. After believing in him, they reflect upon their belief of him and then construct the philosophical arguments for their belief of him. Thus, their belief of him is the cause, and the philosophical arguments are the effect, not the other way around.

We sometimes draw a conclusion and then find premises to justify it. For example, we hate some politicians. As a result, we gather evidence to justify our belief that they are morally bad. Such a cognitive process can also be found in science. In certain cases, scientists first accept a hypothesis and then gather observational data for it. For example, it occurred to Einstein that light bends near the sun, and then scientists collected the observational evidence for the change of relative positions of stars during the solar eclipse in the early 20th century.

2.4. The Neuroscientific Hypothesis

Devout believers tend to have religious experiences. They often fall into religious euphoria when they pray to God or when they listen to their religious leaders' sermons. They feel as if they formed a union with him, i.e., as if they became one with him. After they have the religious ecstasy, they tend to be more charitable and generous to other human beings.

Neuroscientists discovered that multiple regions in the brain (frontal attention regions, medial prefrontal cortex, and nucleus accumbens) work together to give rise to the ineffable joy. Nucleus accumbens is responsible not only for the religious euphoria but also for "drug-induced euphoric states, suggesting common neural mechanisms for these experiences" (Ferguson et al., 2018, p. 104). In plain English, nucleus accumbens lights up when devout believers are in religious euphoria and when drug-users use drugs, such as cocaine.

The neuroscientific hypothesis holds that the multiple regions in the brain are the origin of religious beliefs. Religions would not exist today, had it not been for the activities in those parts of the brain. This view on the origin of religion has the following interesting implication. It will be extremely difficult for disbelievers to persuade devout believers out of religion. Devout believers will not give up belief in God, no matter how powerful philosophical arguments disbelievers might present to them. They will not be swayed by the problems of evil, divine location, divine age, divine foreknowledge, and divine evaluation. They will only feel angry at such problems and at those who advance such problems to them. As far as they are concerned, the euphoric feeling is more valuable than what they can learn from philosophical arguments.

2.4. The Cognitive Hypothesis

The cognitive hypothesis holds that some cognitive features are the origin of religious beliefs.

The cognitive features are postulated in an emerging field of science called "cognitive science of religion (CSR)." CSR attempts to understand religion in terms of the theoretical resources developed in cognitive science. It starts from the following two fundamental assumptions: (i) "whatever it takes to explain how minds work generally will be sufficient to explain how religious minds work" (Lawson, 2000, p. 79). In other words, cognitive mechanisms that generate secular experiences also generate religious experiences, and there is no special cognitive mechanism that is exclusively devoted to generating religious experiences. (ii) The cognitive mechanisms themselves are explained in terms of evolutionary theory. According to CSR, we have the natural inclination to believe in supernatural entities, and religious beliefs are produced by several cognitive features.

One of those cognitive features is the hyperactive agency detection device (HADD) (Guthrie, 1993; Barrett, 2000; Atran, 2002). Due to HADD, we have the tendency to interpret ambiguous objects as cognitive agents. Suppose, for example, that you see an object in a dark forest. It appears to be both a rock and a bear. Under such circumstances, HADD is activated. It takes the perception of the ambiguous object as an input, works on the perception, and then gives out as an output the belief that it is a bear. As a result, you run away from it.

HADD is beneficial for our survival and reproduction. Suppose that the ambiguous object that you see in the dark forest is a rock, but that you take it to be a bear and run away. In such a case, you lose almost nothing. Suppose, by contrast, that it is a bear, but that you take it to be a rock, and that you do not run away. In such a case, you might be lacerated by the bear (Barrett, 2004, p. 31).

Let me give an example of a cloud to illustrate how HADD works. A cloud sometimes makes a figure of a human face or a figure of a human eye. The cloud of a face is an ambiguous object in that it can be interpreted as a mere cloud or as God's face. When you see the cloud of a face in the sky, HADD in your mind kicks in. It takes the perception of the cloud as an input, works on it, and then gives out as the output, viz., the belief that it is his face.

Let me move on to the next cognitive feature, theory of mind (ToM). ToM enables us to read our target agents' minds. Theists believe in God in part because they have ToM in their minds. Believers constantly attempt to read his mind, thinking about how their behavior would affect his mind. For example, they think that he would be happy if they go to church, and he would be unhappy if we do not. Thanks to ToM, believers can attribute mental states, such as joy and anger, to him.

This claim goes hand in hand with the observation on autistic people and women. Autistic people are those who lack the cognitive ability to read others' minds. They cannot tell the difference between human beings and inanimate objects, treating human beings as if they do not have minds. They cannot read others' minds because their ToM malfunctions (Baron-Cohen, Leslie, and Frith, 1985). Not surprisingly, they are less prone to believe in God than other people (Bering, 2002). Women's ToM is more advanced than men's ToM (Baron-Cohen, 2003). As a result, women have a better ability than men to read others' minds, and they are more religious than men (Bloom, 2012, p. 186).

Let me turn to the next cognitive feature, minimally counterintuitive concepts (MCI). The concept of God is minimally counterintuitive in that he is allegedly similar to humans in most respects and dissimilar to humans only in some respects. He looks like a human being, and he can have emotions, such as love, hate, joy, and anger. He is only different from a human being in that he has supernatural powers. It is easier to memorize minimally counterintuitive concepts than intuitive ones or maximally counterintuitive ones (Boyer, 1994, p. 121). If the concept of him were maximally counterintuitive, i.e., if he were too different from humans, we would not believe in him. Suppose, for example, that he looks like a snake, and that he feels joyous when we are disobedient to him. In such a case, no one would believe in him.

The next cognitive feature is dualism, the view that the mind and the body are separate from each other. It implies that the mind can exist without the body and vice versa. A psychological experiment on children suggests that they have the natural propensity to believe that minds and bodies are separate things (Bloom, 2005a). Dualism is apparent in Christianity, according to which our souls will survive the death of our bodies.

According to the cognitive hypothesis, it is due to the aforementioned cognitive features that some people believe in God.

2.5. The Evolutionary Hypothesis

The evolutionary hypothesis holds that religious beliefs originate from the past evolutionary history that our ancestors went through. The past evolutionary history can be fleshed out as follows. In the past, our ancestors did not have the tendency to hold religious beliefs. A variation occurred to them, i.e., some babies were born with the tendency while their competitors were born without it. The tendency was neither an adaptive trait nor a maladaptive trait, and thus the two groups of individuals had the equal chance to survive and reproduce. The tendency was passed on to next generations. As a result, some individuals today have it and hold religious beliefs.

3. The Three Evolutionary Views on Religiosity

The evolutionary hypothesis in Subsection 2.5 above is just one of the three rival evolutionary views on religiosity, being religious. They are the adaptation view, the maladaptation view, and the by-product view.

The adaptation view holds that religiosity is an adaptive trait, i.e., that religiosity makes people more likely to survive and reproduce (Atran, 2002, Wilson, 2002, 2005; Szock and van Eyghen, 2021). The members of the same religious group help one another, thereby increasing the chance to survive and reproduce. As a result, religious individuals do better than nonreligious ones in the battle to survive and reproduce.

By contrast, the maladaptation view holds that religiosity is a maladaptive trait, i.e., that religiosity makes people less likely to survive and reproduce. Believers spend their time and energy in worshiping God, while nonbelievers spend their time and energy in securing resources, such as food and water. As a result, nonreligious individuals do better than religious ones in the battle to survive and reproduce.

Before we move on to the third view, the by-product view, we need to be clear about the concept of spandrel in evolutionary biology. A spandrel is a property that confers neither advantage nor disadvantage to organisms, but it persists because it is a by-product of an adaptive trait (Gould and Lewontin, 1979). What would be an example of a spandrel? Scholars debate over whether music is a spandrel or not. Steven Pinker argues that music is a spandrel, saying that "music is useless" (Pinker, 1997, p. 528). On his account, music neither helps nor hurts survivability and reproducibility. Robin Dunbar objects that music is not a spandrel but an adaptive trait, saying that it plays two useful roles in evolution: "One is its role in mating and mate choice, the other is its role in social bonding" (Dunbar, 2012, p. 202). In simple English, those who sing well have a better chance to mate than those who do not, and music improves the relationship between human beings. As this debate between Pinker and Dunbar indicates, it is difficult to find an example of a spandrel.

Let me use an analogy to illuminate the concept of spandrel.

Imagine that a steam locomotive moves on a railroad. It moves because its engine runs. Without the engine, it would not move. It is the engine that increases the speed of the steam locomotive. By contrast, the smoke that comes out of the engine neither increases nor decreases the speed of the locomotive. The smoke is merely a by-product of the engine that increases the speed of the steam locomotive. Pinker claims that music is like the smoke, while Dunbar claims that it is like the engine.

Now that we are clear about the concept of spandrel, we are ready to move on to the third view on religiosity, the by-product view. It holds that religiosity is a spandrel. To say so implies that religiosity neither increases nor decreases the probability that we survive and reproduce, but that it exists because it is a by-product of adaptive traits: HADD, ToM, MCI, and dualism. Religiosity is a by-product of those traits, just as the smoke is a by-product of the engine (Barrett, 2004; Bloom, 2005b).

How can we adjudicate among the adaptation view, the maladaptation view, or the by-product view? My answer is that the by-product view is the best of all the three views. If the adaptation view were true, only believers should exist. Accordingly, it cannot explain why nonbelievers exist. If the maladaptation view were true, only nonbelievers should exist. Consequently, it cannot explain why believers exist. By contrast, the by-product view can explain why believers and nonbelievers exist. On the by-product view, religiosity is neither an adaptive trait nor a maladaptive trait, and hence both believers and nonbelievers exist.

4. Summary

Some people believe in God, according to the emotional hypothesis, because they are emotionally unstable; according to the philosophical perspective, because they are convinced of the philosophical arguments for his existence; according to the cognitive perspective, because they have the four cognitive features: HADD, ToM, MCI, and dualism. The evolutionary hypothesis holds that the belief of God originates from the past evolutionary history in which religiosity was neither an adaptive trait nor a maladaptive trait.

There are three competing evolutionary views on religiosity: the adaption view, the maladaptation view, and the by-product view. They assert, respectively, religiosity is an adaptive trait, a maladaptive trait, and a by-product of the four cognitive features which are adaptive traits. In my view, the by-product view explains both the existence of believers and the existence of nonbelievers while the other two views cannot.

Study Questions

1. What are the two fundamental assumptions of cognitive science

of religion. What are the four cognitive features that jointly generate religious beliefs? How do you respond to the emotional, philosophical, neuroscientific, and cognitive perspectives on the origin of the belief of God? Are they plausible? Are they compatible or incompatible with each other?

2. Explicate the adaptive view, the by-product view, and the maladaptive view on religiosity. Which of them sounds the most convincing to you? How would adaptation theorists respond to the following objection? Buddhist monks, priests, and nuns do not get married. Some believers avoid eating certain foods, and sacrifice their resources to supernatural beings. Consequently, religiosity decreases the chance that believers survive and reproduce.

References

Atran, S. (2002). *In gods we trust: The evolutionary landscape of religion*. Oxford: Oxford University Press.

Baron-Cohen, S., Leslie, A., and Frith, U. (1985). Does the autistic child have a "theory of mind"? *Cognition*, 21(1), 37-46.

Baron-Cohen S. (2003). The essential difference: The truth about the male and female brain. New York: Basic Books.

Barrett, J. (2000). Exploring the natural foundations of religion. *Trends in Cognitive Sciences*, 4(1), 29-34.

Barrett, J. (2004). Why would anyone believe in God? Walnut Creek, CA: AltaMira Press.

Bentzen, J. (2019). Acts of God? Religiosity and natural disasters across subnational world districts. *The Economic Journal*, 129(622), 2295-2321.

Bering J. (2002). The existential theory of mind. *Review of General Psychology*, 6(1), 3-24.

Bloom, P. (2005a). *Descartes' baby: How the science of child development explains what makes us human*. New York: Basic Books.

Bloom, P. (2005b). Is God an accident? *The Atlantic Monthly* (December).

Bloom, P. (2012). Religion, morality, evolution. *Annual Review of Psychology*, 63(1), 179-199.

Boyer, P. (1994). *The naturalness of religious ideas*. Berkeley: University of California Press.

Chen, D. (2010). Club goods and group identity: Evidence from Islamic resurgence during the Indonesian financial crisis, earlier version with model. *Journal of Political Economy*, 118(2), 300-354.

Dunbar, R. (2012). On the evolutionary function of song and dance. In N. Bannan (Ed.), *Music, language, and human evolution* (pp. 201-214). Oxford: Oxford University Press.

Ferguson, M. A., Nielsen, J. A., King, J. B., Dai, L., Giangrasso, D. M., Holman, R., Korenberg, J. R., & Anderson, J. S. (2018). Reward, salience, and attentional networks are activated by religious experience in devout mormons. *Social Neuroscience*, 13(1), 104-116.

Gould, S. and Lewontin, R. (1979). The spandrels of San Marco and the Panglossian paradigm: a critique of the adaptationist programme. *Proceedings of the Royal Society B: Biological Sciences*, 205(1161), 581-598.

Guthrie, S. (1993). *Faces in the clouds*. New York: Oxford University Press.

Lawson, E. T. (2000). Cognition. In W. Braun and R. McCutcheon (Eds.), *Guide to the study of religion* (pp. 75-84). London: Cassell.

Norris, P. and Inglehart, R. (2004). *Sacred and secular: Religion and politics worldwide*. Cambridge: Cambridge University Press.

Pascal, B. (2018). Pensée. Trans. W. Trotter. Mineola, New York: Dover Publications.

Pinker, S. (1997). *How the mind works*. New York: W.W. Norton & Company.

Szock, K. and van Eyghen, H. (2021). *Revising cognitive and evolutionary science of religion*. Cham: Springer.

Wilson, D. (2002). *Darwin's cathedral*. Chicago: University of Chicago Press.

Wilson, D. (2005). Testing major evolutionary hypotheses about religion with a random sample. *Human Nature*, 16(4), 419-446.

Zuckerman, P. (2008). *Society without God: What the least religious nations can tell us about contentment*. New York: New York University Press.

20 CHAPTER

The Cognitive and Religious Hypotheses

1. Overview

In Chapter 19, we discussed the five hypotheses on where the belief of God came from. One of them is the cognitive hypothesis. In this chapter, I compare it with a new hypothesis that I call "the religious hypothesis," and then argue that the cognitive hypothesis is more plausible than the religious one.

2. The Two Hypotheses

The cognitive hypothesis holds that religious beliefs are caused by the cognitive mechanisms, such as the hyperactive agency detection device, theory of mind, minimally counterintuitive concepts, and dualism. If we did not have the cognitive devices, we would not have religious beliefs

Like the cognitive hypothesis, the religious hypothesis asserts that religious beliefs are produced by the aforementioned cognitive mechanisms. Unlike the cognitive hypothesis, however, it makes an additional claim that God implanted the cognitive devices into our minds. Therefore, it is ultimately he who produces religious beliefs in our minds.

There is an important difference between the cognitive and religious hypotheses. The religious hypothesis is committed to the existence of God, while the cognitive hypothesis is not. Other than that, there is no difference between them.

The religious hypothesis is endorsed by many theistic cognitive scientists of religion, such as Justin Barrett (2004), Kelly Clark & Justin Barrett (2011), and John Calvin (2016, p. 22).

3. Nola's Objection to the Religious Hypothesis

The cognitive and religious hypotheses explain the same religious phenomena: theists hold religious beliefs. Which of the two hypotheses should we choose? Robert Nola (2018, Section 4) presents several reasons for choosing the cognitive hypothesis over the religious hypothesis. Let me discuss two of them that I take to be the strongest ones.

Nola argues that the cognitive hypothesis is simpler than the religious hypothesis. The cognitive hypothesis only postulates the existence the aforementioned cognitive mechanisms, while the religious hypothesis postulates the existence of the cognitive mechanisms and God. It follows that the cognitive hypothesis should "be preferred as the more ontologically parsimonious explainer" (Nola, 2018, p. 88). To put it differently, Ockham's razor favors the cognitive hypothesis over the religious hypothesis.

How would Justin Barrett (2004) respond to Nola's case for the cognitive hypothesis over the religious hypothesis? Barrett is one of the founders of cognitive science of religion. He believes that God endowed us with the aforementioned cognitive devices, i.e., he advocates the religious hypothesis. He would point out that the cognitive and religious hypotheses are compatible with each other, and that we cannot rule out the possibility that God gave us the cognitive mechanisms.

Barrett would admit that the cognitive hypothesis is simpler than the religious hypothesis. However, he would point out that the religious hypothesis explains more phenomena than the cognitive hypothesis. The religious hypothesis explains, while the cognitive mechanism does not, why we have the cognitive mechanisms. According to the religious hypothesis, we have them because God implanted them into our minds. Consequently, it is an open question whether the cognitive hypothesis is better than the religious hypothesis.

Nola might retort that we can use evolutionary theory to explain why we have the cognitive mechanisms. Our ancestors acquired the cognitive mechanisms as a result of variations. The cognitive mechanisms made our ancestors outcompete their rivals in the battle to survive and reproduce, and they were passed on to next generations. We have them for that reason. However, Barrett would also embrace the evolutionary explanation, but would claim that God created the entire evolutionary process, and thus it is ultimately he who created the cognitive mechanisms.

Let me turn to the second reason for choosing the cognitive hypothesis over the religious one. Nola argues that true predictions "cannot be obtained out of the God hypothesis alone" (Nola, 2018, p. 88). In other words, the religious hypothesis alone does not make true predictions. Then, how about the cognitive hypothesis?

It does once it is conjoined with evolutionary theory. Evolutionary theory claims that simple species evolved into complex species, so it predicts that we will find fossils of simple species in old geological strata and the fossils of complex species in young geological strata. This prediction has been confirmed ever since Darwin advanced evolutionary theory in 1859 (Coyne, 2009, p. 18). Therefore, the combination of the cognitive hypothesis and evolutionary theory makes true predictions. So Nola argues.

How would Barrett respond to Nola's foregoing argument? He would object that the religious hypothesis also makes true predictions, once it is conjoined with evolutionary theory. The combination of the religious hypothesis and evolutionary theory predicts, for example, that we will find the fossils of simple species in old geological strata and the fossils of complex species in young geological strata. Therefore, the religious and cognitive hypotheses have equal predictive powers, i.e., none of them is better than the other in terms of predictive powers. So Barrett would reply to Nola.

In sum, the cognitive hypothesis is simpler than the religious hypothesis, but the explanatory scope of the religious hypothesis is wider than that of the cognitive hypothesis, and they tie in terms of predictive powers. In consequence, we have no reason to prefer the cognitive hypothesis to the religious hypothesis.

4. My Objections to the Religious Hypothesis

In this section, I raise five objections to the religious hypothesis that we believe in God because he implanted into our minds the cognitive devices that predispose us to believe in him.

First of all, there are many religions in the world, and they worship different deities: God, Allah, Vishnu, and so forth. Which deity put the cognitive devices into our minds? Theists, such as Barrett, owe us an answer to this question. Of course, he says that God implanted the cognitive devices into our minds. However, theists of other religions would disagree with him.

Suppose that God implanted the cognitive features into our minds, and that as a result, we are predisposed to believe in him. To say so means that we do not have the unlimited free will but the limited free will to choose between believing in him and not believing in him. To use an analogy, we are predisposed to sleep at night and eat food when hungry. To say so means that we do not have the unlimited free will but the limited free will to choose between sleeping and not sleeping at night, and between eating food and not eating food when hungry. In general, our predisposition to do X restricts our freedom to choose between doing X and not doing X.

It is not clear to me what motivated God, an omnibenevolent being, to predispose us to believe in him. If he had not done it, we would enjoy the unlimited free will to choose between believing and disbelieving in him. However, he implanted the cognitive devices into our minds. As a result, we are predisposed to believe in him, and we enjoy less free will to choose between believing and not believing in him. An omnibenevolent being would not restrict our free will. It is mysterious why he restricted our free will, and it is not clear whether we should be thankful to him for restricting our free will.

Theists do not deserve to be rewarded for believing in God, i.e., they do not deserve to be sent to heaven after they die. After all, they believe in him not because they made hard efforts to believe in him but rather because they were predisposed to believe in him. Consider that we are predisposed to sleep at night and to eat when hungry. It is not praiseworthy for us to sleep at night and to eat when hungry because we are predisposed to do so. By parity of reasoning, it is not praiseworthy for theists to believe in him because they are predisposed to do so.

The religious hypothesis is in tension with one of the responses to the problem of divine elusiveness that we discussed in Chapter 5. When challenged to explain why God is elusive, theists say that he is testing us. We would pass his test, if we believed in him despite the fact that he is invisible to us. By contrast, we would fail his test, if we disbelieved in him on the ground that he is invisible to us. Implanting the cognitive devices into our minds is like predisposing us to choose the correct answers over the incorrect ones to questions before we take the exam. One may wonder what the purpose of the exam is and what the purpose of predisposing us to choose the correct answers over the incorrect ones.

It is morally wrong for God to implant the cognitive devices into our minds. To use an analogy, suppose that the president of a country is not popular among his people. Her approval rating is, say, 20%. She implants into the brains of her people some electronic devices that predispose them to like her. As a result, her approval rating surges to 90%. What are we to make of her behavior of implanting the electronic devices into the brains of her people? A natural answer to this question is that it was morally wrong. By parity of reasoning, it was morally wrong for God to implant the cognitive devices into our minds so that we are predisposed to believe in him. In short, to say that he implanted the cognitive devices into our minds involves attributing moral wrongness to him. It is wrong for Barrett (2004), Clark & Barrett (2011), and Calvin (2016, p. 22) to say that he implanted the cognitive devices into our minds.

5. Summary

Why do we believe in God? The cognitive hypothesis holds that we have the cognitive devices that predispose us to believe in him, while the religious hypothesis holds that he implanted into our minds the cognitive devices that predispose us to believe in him. Nola argues that the cognitive hypothesis is simpler than the religious hypothesis, and that the cognitive hypothesis, once conjoined with evolutionary theory, makes true predictions.

Barrett would reply that the religious hypothesis explains, while the cognitive hypothesis does not, why we have the cognitive features, and that the religious hypothesis, once conjoined with evolutionary theory, also makes true predictions.

I raised the five objections to the religious hypothesis. (i) There is an unresolved issue of which deity of many religions in the world implanted the cognitive devices into our minds. (ii) It is not clear why God, an omnibenevolent being, limited human beings' free will to choose between believing in him and disbelieving in him. (iii) Believers do not deserve to go to heaven because they are merely acting in accordance with their natural inclination to believe in him when they believe in him. (iv) Predisposing us to believe in him is like predisposing us to choose correct answers over incorrect ones to questions before we take the exam. (v) It is morally wrong for him to implant the cognitive devices into our minds so that we believe in him.

Study Questions

1. What do the cognitive and religious hypotheses say? How does Nola argue that the cognitive hypothesis is better than the religious hypothesis?

2. How would Berrett respond to Nola's case for the cognitive

hypothesis over the religious hypothesis? Who do you agree with? Why?

References

Barrett, J. (2004). *Why would anyone believe in God?* Walnut Creek, CA: AltaMira Press.

Calvin, J. (2016). *Institutes of the Christian religion*. H. Beveridge (trans.), Ontario, Canada: Devoted Publishing.

Clark, K. and Barrett, J. (2011). Reidian religious epistemology and the cognitive science of religion. *Journal of the American Academy of Religion*, 79(3), 639-675.

Coyne, J. (2009). *Why evolution is true*. Oxford: Oxford University Press.

Nola, R. (2018). Demystifying religious belief. In H. van Eyghen, R. Peels, and G. van den Brink (Eds.), *New developments in the cognitive science of religion: The rationality of religious belief*. (pp. 71-92). Cham: Springer.

CHAPTER

21

Why Disbelieve in God?

1. Overview

Why do some people disbelieve in God? What cognitive mechanism is responsible for their disbelief in him? Just as we need to explain why some people believe in him, so we need to explain why other people disbelieve in him. Just as cognitive scientists postulate the existence of the cognitive mechanisms, such as the hyperactive agency detection device (HADD), to explain why believers exist, so I postulate the existence of a new cognitive mechanism that I call "the reflective device (RD)" to explain why some people disbelieve in him.

2. The Reflective Device

RD enables us to reflect upon evidence and then to adjust our belief system. To adjust our belief system means to form a new belief, to eliminate an old belief, and to change the degree of an existing belief. Suppose, for example, that you see an ambiguous object which appears to be both a snake and a round twig. HADD is activated instantly and then you form a new belief that it is a snake. You get closer to the object and take a hard look at it. RD kicks in instantly and then you replace the old belief that it is a snake with the new one that it is a round twig. Without RD, you would continue to believe that it is a snake.

Suppose that you see a cloud of a face in the sky. Your HADD is activated. It takes the visual stimuli as an input, works on it, and produces an output. The output is the belief that the cloud is God's face. Your RD is also activated. It takes the visual stimuli as an input, works on it, and produces an output. The output is the belief that the cloud accidently formed a figure of a face.

HADD inclines you to believe in God while RD inclines you to disbelieve in him. There is a battle between HADD and RD in your mind. You become a believer or a disbeliever depending on which cognitive device wins. If HADD wins, you become a believer, and if RD wins, you become a disbeliever.

There is a similarity between HADD and RD. They are both cognitive systems that take inputs, work on inputs, and give out outputs. HADD takes the obscure visual image of an ambiguous object as an input, works on it, and then gives out the belief that the ambiguous object is a cognitive agent. In contrast, RD takes the clear visual image of an object as an input, works on it, and then gives out the belief that the object is an inanimate one.

There is a difference between HADD and RD. Philosophical arguments for the existence for God, such as the argument from design and the argument from miracles, fall outside the scope of HADD. In other words, it is false that HADD takes a philosophical argument for the existence of him as an input, works on it, and then produces the belief that he exists. HADD takes only a perception as an input. By contrast, RD takes as an input not only a perception but also a philosophical argument. For example, it takes as an input the problem of evil, works on it, and then produces disbelief in God.

RD proportions not only religious beliefs but also secular beliefs to evidence. For example, suppose that you are a supervisor of two office workers: Jones and Smith. Jones and Smith are coworkers and hence competitors to each other. Jones visits your office and speaks ill of Smith, claiming that Smith committed many wrong actions. However, Jones does not provide any evidence to back up his slander against Smith. In such a case, RD is activated in your mind and then assigns a low probability to the belief that Smith committed many wrong actions. In sum, secular beliefs fall in the scope of RD.

Children's RD is weaker than their HADD. Three-year-old children believe that supernatural agents, such as the Easter Bunny and Santa Claus, are real. Once they reach the age of seven or so, they begin to disbelieve that they are real. In my view, children at the age of seven or so lose their old beliefs in supernatural entities because their RD becomes mature and stronger than their HADD.

My view that RD is responsible for disbelief in God goes hand in hand with a survey on professional philosophers. They are asked whether they endorse atheism, theism, or skepticism (or undecided). The result of the survey is that "atheism 72.8 %, theism 14.6 %, other 12.6 %" (Bourget and Chalmers, 2014, p. 476).

My view that RD is responsible for disbelief in God also goes hand in hand with a survey on elite scientists, the members of the National Academy of Sciences (NAS). In the survey, eminent scientists were asked whether they believed in him and immortality. The survey result is that "Disbelief in God and immortality among NAS biological scientists was 65.2% and 69.0%, respectively, and among NAS physical scientists it was 79.0% and 76.3%" (Larson and Witham, 1998, p. 313).

The majority of professional philosophers and elite scientists are nonbelievers, while the majority of laypeople are believers. A possible explanation of this difference is that the majority of professional philosophers and eminent scientists have better abilities than laypeople to modify their belief systems in light of evidence, i.e., that professional philosophers' and elite scientists' RD is stronger than that of laypeople.

Why do we have RD? An evolutionary answer to this question is as follows. In the distant past, our ancestors did not have RD. A variation occurred to them. Some babies were born with RD. They adjusted their belief systems in light of evidence while their rivals did not. As a result, they rewarded those who deserved to be rewarded and punished those who deserve to be punished, while their rivals did not. They had a better chance to survive and reproduce than their rivals. RD was passed on to next generations. After many generations, our ancestors persisted while their rivals perished. As a result, we have RD.

3. Natural?

Aku Visala and Justin Barrett (2018, p. 69) write that religious beliefs are cognitively natural. To say so means that we are born with cognitive mechanisms, such as HADD and ToM, that give rise to religious beliefs, and that cognitive efforts are not required to form religious beliefs. By contrast, religious disbeliefs are unnatural, which means that we do not have a cognitive mechanism that gives rise to religious disbeliefs, and thus cognitive efforts are required to form religious disbeliefs.

This view about religious beliefs and disbeliefs clashes with my view on religious beliefs and disbeliefs. On my account, just as HADD gives rise to belief in God, so RD gives rise to disbelief in him. Children begin to disbelieve in supernatural agents, such as the Easter Bunny and Santa Claus, at around seven or so, not because they make cognitive efforts to disbelieve in supernatural agents but rather because their cognitive mechanism, RD, becomes mature and predisposes them to disbelieve in supernatural entities.

Why is it that some children at the age of seven or so begin to disbelieve in the Ester Bunny and Santa Claus, but not God? Why do they maintain belief in him? My answer is that they are taught by their parents and other adults that he exists while the Easter Bunny and Santa Claus do not. In addition, they watch their parents and other adults perform religious rituals for him, but not for the Easter Bunny and Santa Claus. It is due to such cognitive inputs that they continue to believe in him, while stop believing in the Easter Bunny or Santa Claus. Without such cognitive inputs, they would stop believing in him, just as they stop believing in the Easter Bunny and Santa Claus.

4. Discussion

Cognitive scientists of religion claim that we have HADD on the ground that the hypothesis that we have HADD explains why we interpret an ambiguous object as an agent and why theists exist. Those who reject the hypothesis have the burden of providing an alternative explanation of why we interpret an ambiguous object as an agent and why theists exist.

Similarly, I claim that we have RD on the ground that the hypothesis that we have RD explains why we interpret a round twig as a round twig after taking a close look at it, why some people disbelieve in God, and why some children at the age of seven or so stop believing in supernatural entities, such as the Easter Bunny and Santa Claus. Those who reject my hypothesis have the burden of providing an alternative explanation of why atheists exist, and why some children stop believing that the Easter Bunny and Santa Clause exist.

The existence of RD poses a problem to theistic cognitive scientists of religion, such as Justin Barrett (2004), Kelly Clark and Justin Barrett (2011), and John Calvin (2016, p. 22). These cognitive scientists of religion claim that God implanted cognitive mechanisms, such as HADD, into our minds. By parity of reasoning, they should also claim that he endowed us with RD. Perverse questions arise to them. Why did he bestow RD on us? Is it fair for him to implant strong RD into disbelievers' minds and then send to them to hell? The answer to this question seems to be "No." After all, disbelievers disbelieve in him not because they intentionally chose to disbelieve in him but rather because RD predisposes them to disbelieve in him and he implanted RD into their minds.

5. Summary

RD enables us to modify our belief system in light of evidence. Just as HADD predisposes us to become theists, so RD predisposes us to become atheists. There is a battle between HADD and RD in our minds. We become theists or atheists depending on which cognitive device wins. Some cognitive scientists of religion claim that religious beliefs are cognitively natural. My view is that if your HADD is stronger than your RD, you become a theist, and religious beliefs are cognitively natural for you, but that if your RD is stronger than your HADD, you become an atheist, and religious disbeliefs are cognitively natural for you. Finally, given that God implanted RD into disbelievers' minds, it is unfair for him to send them to hell.

Study Questions

1. What functions does RD perform? What are similarities and differences between HADD and RD? According to the surveys, most professional philosophers and elite scientists are atheists. Do the surveys support or undermine the hypothesis that RD modifies our belief system in light of evidence?

2. Is RD an adaptive trait? Which do you think is more natural, theism or atheism? Did God endow us with RD? Defend your answer whatever it is.

References

Barrett, J. (2004). Why would anyone believe in God? Walnut Creek, CA: AltaMira Press.

Bourget, D. and Chalmers, D. (2014). What do philosophers believe? *Philosophical Studies*, 170(3), 465-500.

Calvin, J. (2016). *Institutes of the Christian religion*. H. Beveridge (trans.), Ontario, Canada: Devoted Publishing.

Clark, K. and Barrett, J. (2011). Reidian religious epistemology and the cognitive science of religion. *Journal of the American Academy of Religion*, 79(3), 639-675.

Larson, E. and Witham, L. (1998). Leading scientists still reject God. *Nature*, 394(6691), 313-314.

Visala, A. and Barrett, J. (2018). In what sense might religion be natural? In P. Copan and C. Taliaferro (Eds.), *The naturalness of belief: New essays on theism's reasonability* (pp. 67-84). Lanham, MD: Lexington Press.

CHAPTER

22

Why Dogmatic? Why Proselytize?

1. Why Dogmatic?

1.1. Problem

Religious practitioners, those who live religious lives, are dogmatic. As we noted in the previous chapters, the positive arguments for the existence of God are all plagued by objections. Moreover, the problems of evil, divine location, divine age, divine foreknowledge, and divine evaluation indicate that he does not exist. If religious practitioners were exposed to the objections and the problems, they would only be angry at them, and they would stick to belief in him.

Why are religious practitioners dogmatic? Why do they refuse to abandon religious beliefs? This section answers this question in the spirit of cognitive science of religion. The answer that this chapter unfolds conforms to one of the fundamental assumptions of cognitive science of religion: "whatever it takes to explain how minds work generally will be sufficient to explain how religious minds work" (Lawson, 2000, p. 79).

1.2. Wilkins's Answer

According to John Wilkins (2018), religious practitioners are dogmatic for the following reasons:

> If you are challenged in your beliefs, you put at risk your social networks with those who use the silly beliefs you hold as a test of

> inclusion, and therefore risk your social connections. To start again will cost you time, effort and resources that could be better spent. (Wilkins, 2018, p. 110)

In this excerpt, Wilkins makes two interesting claims. (i) If religious practitioners stop believing in God, they might lose their social connections. In plain English, if they abandon religious beliefs, they might lose their friends in their religious institutions. As a result, they are dogmatic.

(ii) Religious practitioners maintain religious beliefs, although religious beliefs are silly, because holding the silly beliefs is a way of passing the test of inclusion. In simple English, religious practitioners accept each other as the members of the same religious group on the ground that they share the silly beliefs. If you accept the silly beliefs, you passed the test, and as a result, you are accepted as a member of the religious group. If you reject the silly beliefs, you failed the test, and as a result, you are rejected as a member of the religious group. Since holding the silly beliefs is a way of passing the test of inclusion, religious practitioners maintain the silly beliefs.

How can we test Wilkins's hypothesis of why religious people are dogmatic? Suppose that there are two groups of religious people. The first group of religious people form a religious community. They regularly go to a religious institution and interact with each other in the religious institution. For example, they eat, sing, dance, and pray together. By contrast, the other group of religious people do not go to a religious institution. They pray to their deity alone at home. If Wilkins's hypothesis were true, the first group of religious people would be dogmatic while the second group of religious people would not be. In Chapter 24, readers will see that his hypothesis passes this test.

13. Possible Responses

How would religious practitioners respond to Wilkins's explanation of why they are dogmatic? If I were a religious practitioner, I would raise the following two objections to it.

(i) There is an alternative explanation: religious practitioners are dogmatic because they pursue truths and they hate to lose truths. As far as they are concerned, their belief in God is true, and to give up their belief in him is to give up the truth. In this sense, they are similar to Galileo. Galileo did not give up the belief that the earth revolves around the sun because he pursued the truth and he hated to lose the truth. As far as he was concerned, his belief that the earth revolves around the sun was true, and to give up his belief was to give up the truth. Just as the desire for the truth was what motivated Galileo to be dogmatic, so the desire for the truth is what motivates religious practitioners to be dogmatic.

(ii) Human beings are, in general, dogmatic. It is wrong to think that only religious practitioners are dogmatic. The dogmatic nature of human beings can be illustrated by the following three examples:

Smokers are more likely to get lung cancer than nonsmokers. Suppose that a group of scientists investigate the causal relationship between smoking and lung cancer, and that they release a study which concludes that smoking makes lung cancer more likely. How would a tobacco company respond to the study? It would hire another group of scientists to undermine the study. This new group of scientists would claim that the evidence that the old group of scientists presented is not enough to establish the causal relationship between smoking and lung cancer, and that we cannot rule out the possibility that there might be another factor responsible for smokers' lung cancer. The tobacco company would cling to its old position that there is no causal relationship between smoking and lung cancer. In sum, the tobacco company is dogmatic.

To take another example, people living near a nuclear power plant suffer from thyroid cancer more than those living far from a nuclear power plant. Suppose that a group of scientists investigate the causal relationship between the nuclear power plant and the thyroid cancer, and that they present some evidence to establish the causal relationship between them. How would the nuclear power plant respond to the study? It would hire another group of scientists to undercut the study. This new group of scientists would claim that the evidence that the old group of scientists presented is not sufficient to establish the causal relationship, and that we cannot rule out the possibility that there might be another factor responsible for the thyroid cancer of those living near the nuclear power plant. As a result, the nuclear power plant would stick to its old position that there is no causal relationship between the nuclear power plant and the thyroid cancer. In short, the nuclear power plant is dogmatic.

The same holds for scientists. Scientists do not abandon their theories despite the evidence to the contrary. Thomas Kuhn (1962/1970) is the first philosopher who brought this aspect of scientists to the fore. In the 16th century, for example, Copernicus advanced the heliocentric system according to which the earth moves around the sun. However, Ptolemaic scientists resisted the heliocentric system and stuck to their geocentric system according to which the sun moves around the earth. According to Kuhn, a scientific revolution is completed, i.e., an old theory is replaced with a new theory, not when scientists of an old theory is persuaded that the old theory is false and a new theory is true, but rather when scientists of the old theory die of old ages, which implies that scientists do not give up their old theories until they die. In short, scientists are dogmatic.

Why are scientists dogmatic about their theories? Why do they resist new theories and adhere to old ones? To give up old theories and embrace new theories is to admit that they wasted their career and to lose their hegemony to their rivals who proposed new theories in their scientific community.

It is an open question, though, whether scientists and religious practitioners are equally dogmatic. It would be an interesting research topic to determine whether they are equally dogmatic or not, or whether religious people are more dogmatic than scientists.

2. Why Proselytize?

2.1. Problem

Religious practitioners are not content with keeping religious beliefs to themselves. They make efforts to proselytize nonbelievers, i.e., to propagate their religious beliefs to nonbelievers. Some missionaries travel to remote areas to spread their religious ideas to the less civilized. Why do religious practitioners proselytize nonbelievers? Why are they engaged in evangelism?

This section answers this question with the use of evolutionary theory and with the use of the concept that Richard Dawkins (1976, p. 249) has developed, viz., the concept of meme. The answers conform to the two fundamental assumptions of cognitive science of religion: (i) cognitive mechanisms that generate secular beliefs also generate religious beliefs. (ii) The cognitive mechanisms themselves are explained in terms of evolutionary theory.

2.2. The Evolutionary Explanation

If you ask believers why they proselytize nonbelievers, they would answer that they do it because they feel that religious beliefs are true and they love nonbelievers. To use an analogy, when you eat a delicious food, the desire arises in your mind to share it with those whom you love. Believers have the desire to share their religious beliefs with those whom they love. If they did not love nonbelievers, they would not make any effort to proselytize them.

In general, we have the natural inclination to share our ideas with others. This natural inclination can be found not only in religion but also in other domains, such as politics and science. The members of the same political party, ruling or opposition, aim to spread their political ideas to others. The same holds for scientists. They present their hypotheses in scientific conferences, and they publish them in journals. These activities indicate that they aim to spread their hypotheses to others. Just like politicians and scientists, religious practitioners aim to spread their ideas to others.

Is the natural inclination to spread ideas to others an adaptive trait or a maladaptive trait? It seems to be an adaptive trait. Some people may share the same idea due to this natural inclination, and they might form a group, whether religious or secular. The members of the same group help each other when they are in trouble. As a result, they have a better chance to survive and reproduce than those who do not form a group. The larger the size of a group is, the more likely it is that a member can receive help from other members in the group.

It is an open question, though, whether scientists and religious practitioners are equally aggressive in their attempts to spread their ideas to the world. It would be an interesting research topic to determine whether they are equally aggressive, or whether religious people are more aggressive than scientists.

23. The Memetic Explanation

A meme is a memorable unit, be it an idea or a piece of language, that is transmitted from person to person (Dawkins, 1976, p. 249). For example, when chemistry teachers say to their students that water is H_2O, they are spreading the meme "Water is to H_2O" to their students. When preachers say to their followers, "Love their neighbors," they are spreading the meme "Love your neighbors" to their followers. The word "meme" comes from the words "memory" and "gene."

A meme contrasts with a gene. Just as genes multiply themselves by the means of sex, so memes multiply themselves by the means of communication. Just as we feel good when the genes in our bodies move to others' bodies, so we feel good when the memes in our minds move to others' minds. For example, singers feel good when others like their songs. Scientists feel good when others accept their hypotheses. Similarly, religious practitioners feel good when nonbelievers accept their religious doctrines.

Organisms and memes are similar to each other in the following respects. Just as organisms go through natural selection, so memes go through natural selection. Organisms compete with one another for survival and reproduction in nature, while memes compete with one another for survival and reproduction in our minds. So nature is the battleground for organisms, while our minds are the battleground for memes. In addition, just as fit organisms defeat unfit ones in the battle to survive and reproduce in nature, so fit memes defeat unfit ones in the battle to survive and reproduce in our minds. Religious beliefs seem to be fit memes, given that they persisted for thousands of years in many people's minds.

According to Dawkins, genes use organisms' bodies and minds to survive and reproduce rather than the other way around. It is wrong to think that organisms use genes to survive and reproduce. It is right to think that the genes in our bodies use our bodies and minds for their survival while we are young, and they move to other bodies before our bodies become too weak to have and raise children. They do so by programming our minds to have sex when we are strong enough to have and raise children. As a result of sex, the genes in our bodies jump from our bodies to our children's bodies. Since genes use our bodies and minds, they are selfish.

Similarly, memes use organisms' bodies and minds to survive and reproduce rather than the other way around. It is wrong to think that organisms use memes to survive and reproduce. It is right to think that the memes in our minds use our bodies and minds to survive and to spread to the world. They move to other people's minds by inducing our minds to communicate with others' minds. As a result of the communication, the memes in our minds jump from our minds to others' minds. Since memes use our bodies and minds, Dawkins would say, they are selfish, just as genes are selfish.

Religious beliefs are memes, just as secular beliefs are memes. Religious memes use religious practitioners' bodies and minds to survive and reproduce rather than the other way around. It is wrong to think that religious people use religious memes to go to heaven. It is right to think that religious memes use religious practitioners' minds and bodies to survive and to spread to the world. They move to nonbelievers' minds by inducing religious practitioners to proselytize nonbelievers. As a result of the proselytization, the religious memes in religious practitioners' minds jump from their minds to nonbelievers' minds.

So what? Proselytization can be seen as the struggle for religious memes to multiply themselves. Dawkins would say that when religious people are engaged in evangelism, religious memes are using their minds and bodies so that they might spread to the world.

3. Summary

All humans are dogmatic, and they are dogmatic because they pursue happiness. If it were blameworthy for religious practitioners to be dogmatic, it would also be blameworthy for all human beings, including scientists, to be dogmatic.

All humans have the instinctive desire to spread their ideas to others. If it were reprehensible for religious practitioners to act on the instinctive desire, it would also be reprehensible for all human beings, including scientists, to act on the desire. The instinctive desire to spread their ideas to others seems to be an adaptive trait. Religious practitioners' attempt to proselytize nonbelievers can be understood as the process in which religious memes use religious practitioners' bodies and minds to multiply themselves.

Study Questions

1. Assess Wilkins's explanation of why religious practitioners are dogmatic. How would religious practitioners respond to his explanation? Can you think of an alternative explanation?

2. Appraise the evolutionary and memetic explanations of why religious practitioners proselytize nonbelievers.

References

Dawkins, R. (1976). *The selfish gene*. Oxford: Oxford University Press.

Kuhn, T. (1962/1970). *The structure of scientific revolutions*. Chicago: University of Chicago Press.

Lawson, E. T. (2000). Cognition. In W. Braun and R. McCutcheon (Eds.), *Guide to the study of religion* (pp. 75-84). London: Cassell.

Wilkins, J. (2018). Why do believers believe silly things? Costly signaling and the function of denialism. In H. van Eyghen, R. Peels, and G. van den Brink (Eds.), *New developments in the cognitive science of religion: The rationality of religious belief* (pp. 109-130). Cham: Springer.

CHAPTER 23

Religious Self-Sacrifices

1. Introduction

Some religious practitioners sacrifice themselves for religious causes. For example, they donate money to their religious institutions, they remain celibate until they die, they scar themselves, and/or they become martyrs. Such religious actions might be called "religious self-sacrifices." Why do religious practitioners make religious self-sacrifices? This chapter answers this question from the perspective of cognitive science of religion (CSR).

CSR is an attempt to understand religion from the perspective of cognitive science. It starts from the two fundamental assumptions. One is that "whatever it takes to explain how minds work generally will be sufficient to explain how religious minds work" (Lawson, 2000, p. 79). The other is that evolutionary theory can explain the cognitive architecture that underlies religious beliefs and actions. Pursuant to these two basic tenets, I explain religious self-sacrifices in terms of a cognitive architecture that underpins both secular and religious self-sacrifices and then explain the cognitive architecture in terms of evolutionary theory. I also introduce Daniel Dennett's (2006) memetic explanation of religious self-sacrifices.

2. The Cognitive Explanation

In CSR, a cognitive feature that is invoked to explain secular behavior is also invoked to explain religious behavior. For example, the same cognitive mechanism, HADD, is invoked to explain not only why we sometimes take a rock to be a bear in a dark forest but also why we sometimes take a cloud of a face to be God's face (Guthrie, 1993; Barrett, 2000; Atran, 2002). The relevant presupposition of this scientific practice is that there is no special cognitive feature for religious behavior, i.e., that there is no cognitive feature that is exclusively responsible for religious behavior.

In this spirit, I explain religious self-sacrifices as follows. Humans have the capacity to delay gratification, i.e., to resist an impulse to take an immediate small pleasure in the hope of taking a distant big pleasure. For example, we tend to save money in the bank instead of spending it in the hope that we might use it in the distant future when we are badly in need of it. In the absence of such hope, we would not save money in the bank. The capacity to repress the present desire is responsible not only for secular self-sacrifices but also for religious self-sacrifices, such as tithing, self-injuring, and martyrdom. After all, religious practitioners make self-sacrifices in the hope that they will be later compensated by God. In the absence of such hope, they would not make self-sacrifices.

My suggestion that the capacity to delay gratification is what underlies religious self-sacrifices goes hand in hand with what the Bible states:

> But when you give to the needy, do not let your left hand know what

> your right hand is doing, so that your giving may be in secret. And your Father who sees in secret will reward you. (Matthew 6:3-4).

My suggestion also goes hand in hand with the fact that humans have religions, but nonhuman animals, such as snakes and pigs, do not. Humans have a higher capacity to delay gratification than nonhuman animals. It is in part due to this difference that humans have religions while nonhuman animals do not.

My explanation of religious self-sacrifices has an interesting philosophical implication. Just as it is rational for college students to work hard in the hope of getting good jobs in the future, so it is rational for religious practitioners to make religious self-sacrifices in the hope of being rewarded by God in the future. A common charge brought to believers in the context of the discussion on Pascal's Wager is that it is selfish for believers to believe in him in the hope that they will be sent to heaven. On my account, just as it is justifiable for college students to resist immediate small pleasure to acquire distant bigger pleasure, so it is justifiable for religious practitioners to resist immediate small pleasure to acquire distant bigger pleasure.

3. The Evolutionary Explanation

It appears initially that the inclination to make religious self-sacrifices is maladaptive, i.e., it decreases the chance for religious practitioners to survive and reproduce, and thus that the inclination should have been weeded out by natural selection. In other words, those who have the inclination should have perished, and no current human being should have the inclination. However, many people have the inclination. Why do such people exist? Why does the inclination still exist? This section aims to answer this question from an evolutionary point of view.

An evolutionary explanation of a psychological property or a behavioral tendency is interesting when it appears initially to be maladaptive, but on close examination, it is adaptive. Let me provide two reasons for thinking that the propensity to make self-sacrifices is such a trait. First, the sacrificial members of a religious group may have the worse chance to survive and reproduce than other members, but as a result of their self-sacrifices, other members have the better chance to survive and reproduce, and the group flourishes. In general, a group which has sacrificial members does better in the battle to persist than another group which does not have sacrificial members, as is well-known in evolutionary biology.

Second, the capacity to delay gratification increases the chance for individuals to survive and reproduce. This claim receives support from a famous psychological experiment called "the Stanford marshmallow experiment" (Mischel, 1970). In the experiment, one marshmallow was put in front of children, and they were told that they could eat it immediately, but they would be given one more marshmallow if they waited for fifteen minutes. Some children yielded to the temptation to eat the first marshmallow and were denied the second marshmallow. Other children resisted the temptation and were given the second marshmallow. A follow-up study on the subjects revealed that those who resisted the temptation received higher SAT scores than those who yielded to the temptation. These psychological studies suggest that the capacity to delay gratification has an adaptative value.

My opponents may raise the following objection. The capacity to delay gratification increases the chance to survive and reproduce when it is exercised to secure secular rewards, but decreases the chance when it is exercised to secure religious rewards, such as going to heaven. For example, working hard to get a job and saving money in the bank for future use increases the chance, but remaining celibate and becoming martyrs decreases the chance. It is not clear why the capacity to delay gratification did not disappear in our evolutionary history.

My response to this possible objection is to say that the capacity to delay gratification can persist insofar as its benefit outweigh its cost. The capacity to delay gratification can be compared to other properties, such as the property of being adventurous. Some individuals, such as Columbus, are adventurous while other individuals are timid. Adventurous individuals enjoy exploring new territories while timid individuals do not. The psychological property is harmful to individuals in that it predisposes them to encounter dangers in new territories. However, it is also helpful to individuals in that it predisposes them to discover new resources in new territories. It can persist insofar as its benefit outweighs its cost. Similarly, the capacity to delay gratification can persist as long as its benefit outweighs its cost.

Imagine that genetic mutations will occur to humans in the future. As a result, some babies will be born, and they will be dissimilar to their parents in that they will delay gratification to secure secular rewards, but they will not delay gratification to secure religious rewards. By contrast, their competitors will be similar to their parents in that they will delay gratification not only to secure secular rewards but also to secure religious rewards. Other things being equal, the humans of the first group will be fitter than those of the second group, which implies that if enough time passes, the first group of humans will persist, but the second group of humans will perish. For now, we do not know whether the aforementioned genetic mutations will occur.

4. Dennett's Memetic Explanation

According to Richard Dawkins (1976, p. 249), a meme is an idea that makes copies of itself in our minds. Suppose, for example, that a believer has the meme that God created the universe, that she says to a nonbeliever that he created the universe, and that the nonbeliever accepts the believer's meme. In this case, the meme has succeeded in multiplying itself. Suppose, by contrast, that the nonbeliever rejects the believer's meme. In such a case, the meme has failed to multiply itself. Some thinkers invoke the concept of meme to explain human behavior.

Dennett (2006) is one of those thinkers. He explains religious self-sacrifices as follows. Religious practitioners' suicidal actions are similar to those of rats whose brains are infected with a parasite called "*Toxoplasma gondii*." If a rat is infected with this parasite, it boldly and fearlessly runs in an open field, and as a result it becomes an easy prey for a cat. Once the cat eats the rat, the parasite gets into the cat's stomach where it reproduces itself.

Dennett writes that just as the parasite induces suicidal actions from rats, so religious memes, such as "Submit yourself to God" and "You will go to heaven, if you kill yourself for God," induce suicidal actions from religious practitioners. Just as the parasite uses rats to reproduce itself, so religious memes use religious practitioners to multiply themselves. Religious memes do not have the malicious intention to use religious practitioners to multiply themselves any more than the parasite has the malicious intention to use rats to reproduce itself.

Since Dennett's explanation of religious self-sacrifices invokes the concept of meme, it can be called "a memetic explanation." How does Dennett's memetic explanation relate to the psychological and evolutionary explanations of religious self-sacrifices that I presented in Sections 2 and 3 above? It is compatible with them. Those who accept the psychological and evolutionary explanations may accept Dennett's memetic explanation.

My objection to Dennett's memetic explanation is that it violates the principle of conservation of mass-energy. An idea does not have mass, and hence it does not have energy pursuant to the equation, $E=mc^2$. It follows that it cannot move a body, which implies that it cannot induce suicidal actions from religious practitioners. Therefore, a meme, religious or secular, is incapable of manipulating a body.

5. Summary

Religious self-sacrifices decrease the chance for religious practitioners to survive and reproduce, but they increase the chance for a religious group to flourish. Religious self-sacrifices are grounded on the capacity to delay gratification. The higher the capacity is, the higher the probability is that humans secure secular goods. It persisted in our evolutionary history because individuals with it were likely to survive and reproduce than those without it. In the future, a genetic mutation might occur. As a result, some humans might delay gratification to secure secular rewards, but not to secure religious rewards. If such a genetic mutation occurs, religious self-sacrifice will disappear. Dennett claims that just as rats' self-sacrificial acts are caused by a parasite, so religious practitioners' sacrificial acts are caused by some religious memes.

Study Questions

1. Explicate the cognitive and evolutionary explanations of religious self–sacrifices. How do you respond to them?

2. Explicate Dennett's explanation of religious self–sacrifices. How do you respond to it?

References

Atran, S. (2002). *In gods we trust: The evolutionary landscape of religion*. Oxford: Oxford University Press.

Barrett, J. (2000). Exploring the natural foundations of religion. *Trends in Cognitive Sciences*, 4(1), 29-34.

Dawkins, R. (1976). *The selfish gene*. Oxford: Oxford University Press.

Dennett, D. (2006). *Breaking the spell: Religion as a natural phenomenon*. New York: Penguin Books.

Guthrie, S. (1993). *Faces in the clouds*. New York: Oxford University Press.

Lawson, E. T. (2000). Cognition. In W. Braun and R. McCutcheon (Eds.), *Guide to the study of religion* (pp. 75-84). London: Cassell.

Mischel, W., & Ebbesen, E. B. (1970). Attention in delay of gratification. *Journal of Personality and Social Psychology*, 16(2), 329-337.

CHAPTER 24

Religious Rituals

1. Introduction

Religious practitioners form religious communities. In religious communities, they perform religious rituals, such as collective praying, dancing, chanting, and fasting. What functions do religious rituals perform? What psychological impacts do the group activities have on religious practitioners? What would be the evolutionary explanation of religious rituals? This chapter answers these questions.

2. The Psychological Functions

If a group of people perform a ritual together, they become emotionally close to one another. Suppose that a man and a woman meet for the first time in a nightclub and dance together. The woman moves as the man leads her to move, and vice versa. If they did these things, they would no longer feel that they are strangers to each other (Bloom, 2010). Just as dancing together in a secular place has the effect of establishing and cementing a bond between secular people, so dancing together in a religious place has the effect of establishing and cementing a bond between religious people. Similar stories can be given of other rituals, such as collective praying, chanting, and fasting.

In general, rituals give rise to the emotion that Émile Durkheim (1912) calls "collective effervescence." Collective effervescence is the euphoria that a group of people have when they perform a ritual together, whether the ritual is secular or religious. Rituals solidify the relationship between the members of the same community and make the community cohesive. A study finds that people tend to donate more money to charities after they perform a ritual together (Wiltermuth and Heath, 2009). The reason seems to be that after performing rituals together, they feel like they become one with others, and as a result they feel more sympathy to others. Another study finds that religious groups that perform costly rituals persist longer than those that do not (Sosis and Bressler, 2003). Costly rituals are those that require a lot of time and energy. Thus, religious groups which spend a lot of time and energy in performing rituals last together longer than those which do not.

Suppose that you are a social believer. You are a member of a religious community. You regularly attend a religious institution, perform religious rituals with others, tithe every month, and so forth. In short, you interact with other believers. If so, you are more likely to donate money to charities and to support suicide bombings than nonbelievers. In other words, your interaction with others in a religious community has an impact on your moral life, making you morally better or worse than nonbelievers (Ginges et al., 2009).

By contrast, suppose that you are a lonely believer. You believe in God and pray to him alone at home. You are not a member of a religious community. You do not attend a religious institution, do not perform religious rituals with others, do not tithe every month, etc. In short, you do not interact with other believers. If so, you are no more likely to donate money to others and no more likely to support suicide bombings than nonbelievers. To put it differently, your religious beliefs, which are not accompanied by religious rituals, have no impact on your moral life, making you neither morally better nor worse than nonbelievers (Ginges et al., 2009).

So what? What makes a difference to our moral lives is not religious beliefs but rather religious actions (Bloom, 2012, p. 192). Only when religious people form a community and interact with one another, can they be morally better or worse than nonbelievers.

There are other interesting facts about religious rituals. You tend to become more religious when you watch other believers perform religious *rituals* than when you watch others merely *speak* what they believe. Their actions have a more powerful impact on your mind than do their words. In addition, you tend to become more religious when you watch *prestigious* people perform religious rituals than when you watch ordinary people perform religious rituals (Henrich and Gil-White, 2001). Finally, you tend to become more religious when you watch *costly* religious rituals than when you watch uncostly religious rituals (Sosis and Alcorta, 2003).

3. The Evolutionary Explanation

Why do religious people perform rituals? Why do they feel

euphoria when they perform rituals? An evolutionary answer to this question goes as follows. In the distant past, our ancestors did not perform rituals. A variation occurred to them, i.e., some babies were born with the propensity to perform group rituals. They felt good when they performed group rituals. The propensity was an adaptive trait, i.e., those who had the propensity had a better chance to survive and reproduce than those who did not. The propensity was passed on to next generations. As time passed, those who had the propensity persisted, while those who did not perished. As a result, we have the propensity today.

What would be the reason for thinking that the propensity to perform group rituals was an adaptive trait? Our ancestors and their competitors lived in the environment where there were predators, such as tigers and wolves. Our ancestors formed a group and performed rituals together as a result of the propensity, while their competitors did not. Our ancestors were less likely to fall prey to predators than their competitors.

A problem arose when our ancestors formed a group, viz., some members betrayed the group. Such members are called "cheaters," "free-riders," or "defectors" in evolutionary biology. How could our ancestors know whether a particular member was a cheater or not? In other words, how could they know which members were loyal to the group and which other members were disloyal to the group? In addition, how could they make sure that the members of their group did not betray their group?

Performing rituals together was an evolutionary solution to these two problems. Active participation in group rituals was a way to express commitment to a group. If a member of a group had actively participated in group rituals, other members could have known that the member was loyal to the group. If another member of a group had not actively participated in group rituals, other members could have known that the member was not loyal to their group. In short, our ancestors distinguished between loyal and disloyal members by observing whether they actively participated in group rituals. In addition, our ancestors instilled loyalty into their minds and reduced the number of defectors by performing rituals together.

The propensity to perform group rituals is manifest in diverse forms today. For example, we sing the national anthem at the beginning of a ceremony in schools and in government offices. Such a ritual is intended to instill patriotism into us, i.e., to make sure that we do not betray our country. To take another example, military cadets pledge allegiance to their country when they are commissioned as military officers. Such a ritual is also intended to instill patriotism into their minds. Those who refuse to go through the ritual are sending a message to others that they are not loyal to their country.

The same holds for religious rituals. Those who actively participate in religious rituals are likely to be loyal to their religious group. By regularly performing costly rituals, they are implicitly sending a message to other members, although they are not aware, that they are strongly committed to their religious group, and that they will not betray their religious group. Those who do not actively participate in religious rituals are implicitly sending a message to other members, although they are not aware, that they are not strongly committed to their religious group. The degree of participation in group rituals is proportional to the degree of loyalty and to the degree of trustworthiness. Therefore, religious rituals "serve as hurdles that weed out the uncommitted" (Bloom, 2012, p. 186).

Our Paleolithic ancestors lived in forests and fields, hunting down animals and picking up fruit. They frequently encountered rival humans and predators. In Paleolithic environments, those who formed cohesive groups had a better chance to survive and reproduce than those who did not. In civilized societies today, however, those who form cohesive groups have only a slightly better chance for their survival and reproduction than those who do not. We are by and large independent of one another in civilized societies.

4. Summary

Religious rituals perform the function of establishing and strengthening the bond between the members of a religious group. Social believers are morally better or worse than nonbelievers, while lonely believers are neither more morally better nor morally worse than nonbelievers. We have the propensity to perform rituals, religious and secular, because it was an adaptive trait. It performed not only the function of solidifying the relationship between the members of a group but also the function of revealing who are loyal members and who are disloyal members of a group. Religious rituals are a vestige of our Paleolithic ancestors' propensity to perform group rituals.

Study Questions

1. Provide some examples of secular and religious rituals. What functions do secular and religious rituals perform? In other words, what impact do secular and religious rituals have on people?

2. Explain why religious practitioners perform rituals from an evolutionary point of view. Suppose that there are two countries. One country is religious while the other is not, and other conditions of the two countries are equal. Which country will last longer? Defend your answer whatever it is.

References

Bloom P. (2010). How pleasure works: The new science of why we like what we like. New York: Norton.

Bloom, P. (2012). Religion, morality, evolution. *Annual Review of Psychology*, 63(1), 179–199.

Durkheim, E. (1912/1995). The elementary forms of religious life. New York: Free Press.

Ginges, J., Hansen, I., and Norenzayan, A. (2009). Religion and support for suicide attacks. *Psychological Science*, 20(2), 224–230.

Henrich, J. and Gil-White, F. (2001) The evolution of prestige: freely conferred status as a mechanism for enhancing the benefits of cultural transmission. *Evolution and Human Behavior*, 22(3), 1–32.

Sosis, R. and Alcorta, C. (2003) Signaling, solidarity, and the sacred: The evolution of religious behavior. *Evolutionary Anthropology*, 12(6), 264–274.

Sosis, R. and Bressler, E. (2003). Cooperation and commune longevity: A test of the costly signaling theory of religion. *Cross-Cultural Research*, 37(2), 211–239.

Wiltermuth, S. and Heath, C. (2009). Synchrony and cooperation. *Psychological Science*, 20(1), 1–5.

25 CHAPTER

Religious Euphoria

1. A Puzzle

Suppose that you are a deeply religious person. When you pray to God, you have a spiritual experience. You feel as if you formed a union with him, i.e., you became one with him, and you have an intense sweet feeling. In short, you are in the state of religious euphoria.

An interesting question arises. Why do religious people have the capacity to have a religious euphoria? It appears at least initially that the capacity to have the spiritual experience is a maladaptive trait, i.e., that it decreases the probability that religious people survive and reproduce. After all, if they pursue religious euphoria instead of worldly power, money, and fame, they have less chance to survive and reproduce. Accordingly, it is a mystery from an evolutionary point of view why they have the capacity to have a religious euphoria.

In this chapter, I answer this question in the spirit of cognitive science of religion. Cognitive science of religion is built upon the following two fundamental assumptions. The first one is that (i) "whatever it takes to explain how minds work generally will be sufficient to explain how religious minds work" (Lawson, 2000, p. 79). To put it differently, the cognitive mechanism that produces secular experiences also produces religious experiences. The second one is that the cognitive mechanism should be explained in terms of evolutionary theory. My answer to the question above operates under these two fundamental assumptions.

2. The Evolutionary Explanation

What would be the reason for thinking that the capacity to have a religious euphoria is an adaptive trait?

Imagine that there was a group of human beings in the Paleolithic Age. There was a group leader and her followers in the group. You were one of her followers. You knew that if she liked you, she would grant you a high position in the group, and that if she hated you, she would ostracize and persecute you. As a result, you made an effort to establish and maintain a good relationship with her. For example, you gave food to her, and you promised her that you would be loyal to her, and that you would fight against those who were disloyal to her. As a consequence, you formed a special relationship with her. The special relationship helped your survivability and fertility. You had a sweet feeling when you thought that you were in a special relationship with her.

Let me turn to a current society. Suppose that there are one hundred lawmakers in your country, and that you are one of them. You think that you are in a special relationship with the president of your country while other lawmakers are not. For example, you and your president graduated from the same high school, and thus you can call her at any time with your cell phone. In such a situation, you would be more likely to get a leadership position in the legislative branch of your government or a high position in the administrative branch of your government. As a result, you have a sweet feeling when you think that you are in a special relationship with your president.

The foregoing two imaginary stories indicate that we tend to have a sweet feeling when we think that we are in a special relationship with the powerful. The emotive tendency does not discriminate between powerful humans and deities. That is, we have a sweet feeling not only when we think that we are in a special relationship with powerful humans but also when we think that we are in a special relationship with powerful deities (Seokhyun An, Personal Communication). In addition, it does not matter whether we are really in such a relationship with the powerful. As long as we *think* that we are in such a relationship with the powerful, we fall into euphoria.

Why do we have the emotive tendency to be in euphoria when we think that we are in a special relationship with the powerful? An evolutionary answer goes as follows. In the distant past, our ancestors did not have the emotive tendency. A variation occurred to them, i.e., some babies were born with the emotive tendency. They were more likely to receive benefits from their leaders than their competitors who did not have the emotive tendency. The former and the latter grew up and had their own children. The former's children had the emotive tendency while the latter's children did not. After many generations, those who had the emotive tendency persisted, while those who did not perished. For this reason, we have the emotive tendency today.

3. Why More Intense?

Why is a religious euphoria more intense than a secular euphoria? Why do religious people enjoy a more intense sweet feeling than secular people do?

There are diverse leaders in a secular society today, be they the president of a country, the chairperson of a political party, a chairperson of a private company, the president of a university, a military officer in charge of enlisted soldiers, a team leader of a government office, the president of a news agency, the president of a bank, the head of a hospital, or a judge in court. These leaders have the powers of diverse degrees.

The degree of your sweet feeling is proportional to the degree of your leader's power you think that she has. That is, the more power you think your leader has, the more intense sweet feeling you have. For example, you have a more intense sweet feeling when you think that you are in a special relationship with the president of your country than when you think that you are in a special relationship with the team leader of a government office.

In addition, secular leaders might be defeated by their secular rivals. For example, the president of your country might be defeated by the leader of the opposition party or by the president of another country. You have a less sweet feeling when you fear that your leader might be defeated by her secular rival than when you are confident that she will not be defeated by her secular rival.

Secular leaders sometimes betray their followers. Let me provide two examples. First, Bangweon Lee (1367–1422), the third king of the Joseon Dynasty (1392–1910) in the Korean Peninsula, used his followers to become a king. After he came to the throne, however, he killed many of his followers to strengthen his power. Second, your boss orders you to do something illegal. You do what she ordered you to do. Unfortunately, you and your boss are caught by the police. To your surprise, your boss tells the police that she did not order you do what you did, and that you did what you did voluntarily. You are jailed but she is not. You cannot have a sweet feeling when you fear that your secular leader might betray you.

How does God differ from secular leaders? He is allegedly much more powerful than secular leaders and his rival deities. More importantly, he is allegedly omnibenevolent, which implies that he allegedly does not betray his followers. For these reasons, religious believers have a more intense sweet feeling when they think that they are in a special relationship with him than when they think that they are in a special relationship with a secular leader.

4. Obedient vs. Disobedient Individuals

There are diverse individuals in a society. To simplify the matter, some individuals have the temperament to be obedient to an existing authority, while other individuals have the temperament to be disobedient to the existing authority. Obedient individuals seldom criticize the existing leader, while disobedient individuals often criticize the existing leader. Who are more adaptive individuals? It is not clear what the correct answer to this question is.

It appears that obedient individuals are fitter than disobedient individuals. Obedient individuals usually have a good relationship with the existing leader. As a result, they live lives of high socioeconomic status. Disobedient individuals usually have a bad relationship with the existing leader. As a result, they live lives of low socioeconomic status. For example, Korea was Japan's colony from 1910 to 1945. Pro-Japanese Koreans lived easy lives while anti-Japanese Koreans lived hard lives during and after the colonial period.

However, this view is undermined by counterexamples. Consider, for example, the political situation in France in the 1940s. Germany invaded France in 1940. Some French people supported the Nazis, while other French people opposed the Nazis. The former had easy lives, while the latter had hard lives. The U.S. joined the Second World War in 1941. With the help of the U.S., a French general, Charles de Gaulle (1890-1970), expelled German troops from France. His government severely punished pro-Nazi French people. About 1500 of them were executed, and about 10,000 of them were convicted. Such an episode undermines the view that the temperament to be obedient to an existing authority is an adaptive trait.

In nature, it is to some extent a matter of luck which organisms live and which organisms die. For example, a large meteorite hit the earth about 65 million years ago. As a result, the temperature of the earth dropped significantly. Before the event, dinosaurs were fitter than mammals. After the event, however, mammals were fitter than dinosaurs. This example illustrates that as the environment changes, fit organisms may become unfit, and that unfit organisms may become fit.

So what? It is also to some extent a matter of luck which individuals survive and reproduce, obedient or disobedient ones. This conclusion goes hand in hand with the examples of Korea and France.

5. The Final Thought

In this section, I argue that the temperament to be obedient to an existing leader is overall more advantageous for survival and reproduction than the temperament to be disobedient to the existing leader.

We do not treat the strong and the weak equally. We tend to be more respectful to the strong than to the weak. For example, we tend to be more respectful to our superiors than to our subordinates in our workplaces. We have this tendency because it was an adaptive trait. Our Paleolithic ancestors who had it were fitter than their competitors who had the tendency to treat the strong and the weak equally. It follows that the temperament to be obedient to an existing leader is more fitness-conducive than the temperament to be disobedient to the existing leader.

What is an implication of this conclusion? Those who have the temperament to be obedient to the powerful, be they powerful humans or deities, are more likely to survive and reproduce than those who have the temperament to be disobedient to the powerful. Those who pursue the aforementioned euphoria are more likely to be obedient to an existing authority than those who do not pursue it. As a result, the former are more likely to enjoy a high socioeconomic status than the latter.

6. Summary

The capacity to have a euphoria is fitness-conducive. We fall into euphoria when we think that we are in a special relationship with the powerful, be they powerful humans or deities. Being obedient and loyal to the powerful is a way to form and maintain the special relationship with the powerful. The special relationship leads to a high socioeconomic status. Therefore, we acquire a high socioeconomic status as a result of pursuing a euphoria.

Study Questions

1. Provide the evolutionary explanation of why religious people fall into a religious euphoria when they think that they are in a special

relationship with God. Provide your own example in which some people live happy lives as a result of obeying an existing leader, and your own example in which some people live unhappy lives as a result of disobeying an existing leader. Why is a religious euphoria more intense than a secular euphoria?

2. Which is more advantageous for survival and reproduction, the temperament to be obedient to an existing leader or the temperament to be disobedient to an existing leader? Provide your own example to justify your answer whatever it is. Why do some South Koreans have a euphoria when they think that South Korea is in a special relationship with the U.S.? Is the sweet feeling justifiable? Can the U.S. be replaced with Russia or China? If not, why not? If so, why?

Reference

Lawson, E. T. (2000). Cognition. In W. Braun and R. McCutcheon (Eds.), *Guide to the study of religion* (pp. 75-84). London: Cassell.

CHAPTER 26

The Impact of Religion on Morality

1. Introduction

Does religion make us morally better or worse? Some claim that religion has a positive impact on morality, and thus theists are morally better than atheists. Others claim that religion has a negative impact on morality, and thus atheists are morally better than theists. This chapter explores the issue of whether religion is helpful or harmful to our moral lives.

2. Religious vs. Secular Beliefs

Religion seems to make us morally better. Consider the belief that God, an omniscient deity, watches us at every moment. This belief discourages us from committing (morally) wrong acts, such as cheating, stealing, and killing (Bering, 2006, 2011; Norenzayan and Shariff, 2008). The same holds for the religious belief that heaven and hell exist (Johnson, 2005; Johnson and Bering, 2006). In a psychological experiment (Shariff and Norenzayan, 2007), subjects are reminded of God, and as a result they are less prone to commit wrong acts and tend to be more generous to others.

However, some secular beliefs also seem to make us morally better. Consider the secular belief that if you commit a crime, you will be punished by the government, and that if you commit a wrong act, you will be criticized by others. This secular belief also discourages you from committing wrong acts. In a psychological experiment (Shariff and Norenzayan, 2007), subjects are reminded of the police and civic responsibility, and as a result they are less prone to commit wrong acts and tend to be more generous to others.

In short, just as some religious beliefs make us morally better, so some secular beliefs make us morally better.

3. Religious vs. Secular Communities

Religion boosts altruism. There are religious charities, such as the Salvation Army, in the U.S. They receive donations from people and then use donations to help the needy. In addition, some states are more religious than other states in the U.S. According to Internal Revenue Service, people in more religious states donate more to charities than those in less religious states (Brooks, 2006, p. 23). Therefore, believers are more altruistic toward others than are nonbelievers.

However, a study suggests that the least religious countries are morally better than more religious countries. Denmark and Sweden are "the least religious countries in the world" (Zuckerman, 2008, p. 2). Danes and Swedes "don't worship Jesus or Vishnu, don't revere sacred texts, don't pray, and don't give much credence to the essential dogmas of the world's great faiths" (Zuckerman, 2008, p. 2). Yet, Denmark and Sweden enjoy "the lowest violent crime rates in the world" (Zuckerman, 2008, p. 2). Therefore, religion is not required to live in "an earthly heaven" (Zuckerman, 2008, p. 2).

4. Moral Guidance

Religion seems to make us morally better. When you do not know whether certain actions are right or wrong, you can consult the Bible. The Bible tells you which actions are right and which actions are wrong. For example, it tells you to "love your enemies and pray for those who persecute you" (Matthew 5:44). It also tells you not to commit adultery. Thus, it provides us with the guidance on what to do and what not to do.

However, studies on babies and toddlers suggest that they know what actions are right and wrong, and thus that it is wrong to suggest that "morality requires religion" (Bloom, 2012, p. 188). Paul Bloom (2013) reports an experiment on a one-year-old baby. The baby watches a puppet show in which there are three puppets. The puppet in the middle plays with its ball and then rolls it to the puppet on the right. The puppet on the right plays with it and then rolls it back to its owner, the puppet in the middle. The puppet in the middle now rolls it to the puppet on the left. The puppet on the left plays with it and then runs away with it. After the show, the baby is asked to choose between the right and left puppets; the baby chooses the right puppet over the left one, and even smacks the left one. This experiment shows that babies know who are good guys and who are bad guys independently of religion. Thus, morality is prior to religion.

Moreover, scriptures have some gruesome verses. For example, the Quran states that you should kill disbelievers "wherever you find them" (2:191). In other words, Muslims should kill those who do not believe in Allah. In the Bible, Moses orders the military offices of Israelites to slaughter Midianites, saying that they should "kill all the boys, as well as every woman who has had relations with a man, but spare for yourselves every girl who has never had relations with a man" (Numbers 31:17-18). In other words, Israelites should kill all Midianites except virgins, and they can use the virgins for their own purposes. It appears that God commands a genocide against heretics, those who have a different religion.

The foregoing example of the genocide illustrates that the moral guidance that the Bible offers us is not perfect, and that not all verses in the Bible are trustworthy. As a consequence, we should think for ourselves about which verses in the Bible are trustworthy, and which verses in the Bible are not, instead of blindly trusting every verse in the Bible. To go further, we have to think for ourselves which actions are right and which actions are wrong, and we do not need to consult the Bible to determine whether an action is right and wrong.

The church takes positions on such moral issues as same-sex marriage, abortion, and the death penalty. Specifically, the church opposes same-sex marriage, abortion, and the death penalty. The church might be right or wrong on these moral issues. We may take into account church's opinions about the moral issues. However, it is ultimately we who should decide for ourselves whether those actions are right or wrong. If our decisions are right, we will be praised. If our decisions are wrong, we will be blamed. Whatever the outcome might be, we should make decisions for ourselves and take responsibility for our decisions.

5. The Power of Religion

Some theists commit atrocities, such as holy wars, human sacrifices, witch-hunts, and suicide bombings. Their behaviors are grounded in their scriptures. For example, the Quran states that you should "kill polytheists" (9:5), and that "Disbelief is worse than killing" (2:191). To state it otherwise, not to believe in Allah is more blameworthy than to kill human beings. The Bible states, "Whoever sacrifices to any god other than the LORD must be destroyed" (Exodus 22:20). To put it otherwise, you should kill heretics. The Bible also states, "Do not allow a sorceress to live" (Exodus 22:18). To put it differently, you should kill witches. Suicide bombers believe "that duty to God exceeds all other priorities, and that martyrdom in his service will be rewarded in the gardens of Paradise" (Dawkins, 2006, p. 348).

For this reason, Blaise Pascal (1623-1662), a mathematician and philosopher, says, "Men never do evil so completely and cheerfully as when they do it from religious conviction" (Pascal, 2018, p. 265). Similarly, Steven Weinberg (1933-2021), a theoretical physicist, says, "With or without religion, good people can behave well and bad people can do evil; but for good people to do evil - that takes religion" (Weinberg, 1999). In other words, religion is required for good people to do evil things. Therefore, religion is harmful to our moral lives.

Freeman Dyson (1923-2020), another theoretical physicist, counters that "for bad people to do good things that takes religion" (Dyson, 2006). To put it another way, religion is required for bad people to do noble things. Religious conviction can fuel love for others, and the desire to go to heaven can motivate bad people to do good things. Even heinous criminals in a death-row might submit to God, and as a result, they might become good people. Therefore, religion is helpful to our moral lives.

What can we conclude? It might be that the negative impact of religion on morality is more powerful than is the positive impact of religion on morality, and hence that religion overall makes us morally worse. Or it might be that the positive impact of religion on morality is more powerful than is the negative impact of religion on morality, and hence that religion makes us morally better. It would be an interesting research topic to determine which impact is more powerful, the negative one or the positive one. In any event, Weinberg and Dyson would agree that religion has a powerful impact on our moral lives (Bloom, 2012, p. 195).

6. Division vs. Unification

Religion promotes division among humans. The Bible says, "Love your neighbor as yourself" (Leviticus 19:18). You may think that "your neighbor" in this sentence refers to everyone in the world, and hence that the sentence means that we should love all human beings in the world. On close examination, however, "your neighbor" is "intended to apply only to other Israelites" (Graham and Haidt, 2010, p. 144). Hence, the sentence means that Israelites should love each other, but not non-Israelites. The Quran is similar to the Bible on this count. The Quran says, "Do not take Jews and Christians as allies" (5:51). To put it otherwise, Muslims should not love Jews and Christians. In consequence, we can say that religion has the "power to divide people, to motivate hatred toward heretics and apostates, and to fuel violence and genocide and war" (Bloom, 2012, p. 190).

However, we can also say that religion promotes unification, i.e., that it also dissolves boundaries among human beings (Bloom, 2012, p. 193). For example, the Muslims in the Middle East and the Muslims in Xinjian, the northwestern part of China, are citizens of different countries, but they share the same religion. As a result, they think that they are brothers and sisters to each other. So do Christians. For instance, there is some animosity between Koreans and Japanese. There could be less animosity between some Koreans and some Japanese who attend the same church. In the same church, they could form a single religious community, thinking that they are all God's children. Therefore, religion is "a mechanism to bring people together" (Bloom, 2012, p. 194).

7. Summary

The religious belief that God watches us discourages us from committing wrong acts. However, so does the secular belief that other people may watch us. In the U.S., more religious states are more altruistic than less religious states. However, Denmark and Sweden enjoy the lowest crime rates in the world, although they are atheist countries. Scriptures do not provide us with the perfect moral guidance, given that it encourages us to commit wrong acts toward heretics and apostates. Religion has two faces in that it can make some good people bad and some bad people good, and in that it promotes division and unification among people.

Study Questions

1. Weinberg claims that religion is required for good people to do bad things. Dyson counters that religion is required for bad people to do good things. Does religion make us morally better or worse? Theists consult scriptures to determine whether an action is right or wrong. How do you respond to them?

2. Which country is morally better, a religious country or a secular country? Does religion divide or unify people? Would we be morally better or worse without religion? You may provide your own examples or an account of your personal experience to answer these questions.

References

Bering, J. (2006). The folk psychology of souls. *Behavioral and Brain Sciences*, 29(5), 453-498.

Bering, J. (2011). *The belief instinct: The psychology of souls, destiny, and the meaning of life*. New York: Norton.

Bloom, P. (2012). Religion, morality, evolution. *Annual Review of Psychology*, 63(1), 179-199.

Bloom, P. (2013). *Just babies: The origins of good and evil*. New York: Broadway Books.

Brooks, A. (2006). *Who really cares: The surprising truth about compassionate conservatism*. New York: Basic Books.

Dawkins, R. (2006). *The God delusion*. New York: Bantam.

Dyson, F. (2006). Religion from the outside. N.Y. Rev. Books, June 22.

Graham, J. and Haidt, J. (2010). Beyond Beliefs: Religions bind individuals into moral communities. *Personality and Social Psychology Review*, 14(1), 140-150.

Johnson, D. (2005). God's punishment and public goods: A test of the supernatural punishment hypothesis in 186 world cultures. *Human Nature*, 16(4), 410-446.

Johnson, D. and Bering, J. (2006). Hand of God, mind of man: Punishment and cognition in the evolution of cooperation. *Evolutionary Psychology*, 4(1), 219-233.

Norenzayan, A. and Shariff, A. (2008). The origin and evolution of religious prosociality. *Science*, 322(5898), 58-62.

Pascal, B. (2018). Pensée. Trans. W. Trotter. Mineola, New York: Dover Publications.

Shariff, A. and Norenzayan, A. (2007). God is watching you: Priming God concepts increases prosocial behavior in an anonymous economic game.

Psychological Science, 18(9), 803-809.

Weinberg, S. (1999). *A designer universe? (Did the universe have a cosmic designer?)*. N.Y. Rev. Books 46: 46-48. https://www.physlink.com/education/essay_weinberg.cfm

Zuckerman, P. (2008). *Society without God: What the least religious nations can tell us about contentment*. New York: New York University Press.

CHAPTER

27

Religious Wars

1. Preamble

There were many religious wars in the human history. The most famous one is the Crusades that occurred from the 11th to 13th centuries. Scriptures fuel hatred toward heretics. The Bible says, for example, "Whoever sacrifices to any god other than the LORD must be destroyed" (Exodus 22:20). The Quran also states that you should "kill the polytheists wherever you find them" (9:5). Why do scriptures fuel hatred toward heretics? Why do religious wars occur? This chapter aims to answer these questions from the perspective of cognitive science of religion.

2. The Paleolithic Age

When asked to explain why current humans have a certain property, evolutionary biologists imagine what would have happened to our ancestors who had the property and to their competitors who did not have the property in the Paleolithic Age. Why in the Paleolithic Age? Our Paleolithic ancestors were genetically identical with us, but they lived in the environments that were quite different from current environments. Therefore, we should ponder whether the property is adaptive or maladaptive not in current environments but rather in Paleolithic environments.

Our Paleolithic ancestors were hunter-gatherers. They traveled around in groups in search of the resources, such as animals and fruit. Each group consisted of 50 people or so. They were family members, relatives, and acquaintances to each other. They helped each other in the battle to survive and reproduce. Imagine that a traveling group encountered another group in a certain place. They were interested in the same resources, but the resources were not enough to sustain both groups. Moreover, there was no government that could resolve the conflict between them. Consequently, a war between them was inevitable.

According to Steven Pinker (2011, pp. 48-50), 15% of humans were murdered by other humans in the Paleolithic Age, whereas only 3% of humans were murdered by other humans in the 20th century when there were the First World War and the Second World War. It follows that our Paleolithic ancestors were brutal, and wars between traveling groups were prevalent and perennial phenomena in the Paleolithic Age.

3. Evolutionary Explanation

Let me first clarify two terms: "in-group members" and "out-group members." Suppose that there was a group of humans traveling in search of animals and fruit in the Paleolithic Age. The members of the group were in-group members to each other. To say so means that they were family members, relatives, and acquaintances to each other, and that they regularly interacted with each other in the battle to survive and reproduce. They encountered another group of traveling humans. The members of the first group and the members of the second group were out-group members to each other. To say so means that they were strangers to each other, and that they did not regularly interact with each other in the battle to survive and reproduce.

Let me define another two terms: "parochialists" and "egalitarians." In the Paleolithic Age, parochialists were those who were friendly to in-group members but unfriendly to out-group members (Rusch, 2014, pp. 1-2). They felt sympathy to in-group members, but not to out-group members. By contrast, egalitarians were those who were friendly to both in-group and out-group members. They felt sympathy not only to in-group members but also to out-group members.

Parochialists were friendly to in-group members. As a result, they received benefits from in-group members, i.e., they were rewarded by in-group members. For example, they had babies together with in-group members. They were unfriendly to out-group members. As a result, they attacked out-group members and secured resources for themselves and in-group members. They did not regularly interact with out-group members, and thus they were not retaliated against by out-group members.

Egalitarians were friendly to in-group members. As a result, they received benefits from in-group members. However, they were also friendly to out-group members. As a result, they did not attack out-group members. They did not receive benefits from out-group members because they did not regularly interact with out-group members.

Who were fitter individuals between parochialists and egalitarians in the Paleolithic Age? My answer is that parochialists were fitter than egalitarians. Imagine that they existed simultaneously in the Paleolithic Age and competed with each other in the battle to survive and reproduce. There were not enough resources to sustain both parochialists and egalitarians. Parochialists could secure more resources than egalitarians. As a result, parochialists were more likely to survive and reproduce than egalitarians. Not surprisingly, parochialists take up a far more portion of the general population than egalitarians today.

4. The Application to Wars

Why do wars occur? This question can be answered from both psychological and evolutionary points of view. A psychological answer is that we have the psychological propensity to be friendly to in-group members but unfriendly to out-group members, and the psychological propensity underlies wars. An evolutionary answer is, to make the long story short, that the psychological propensity was an adaptive trait in the Paleolithic Age. For this reason, we have the psychological propensity, and the psychological propensity underlies wars.

The foregoing psychological and evolutionary explanations apply equally to both secular and religious wars. Religious believers are friendly to in-group believers but unfriendly to out-group believers, not because they have a distinctive cognitive feature that predisposes them to be friendly to in-group believers but unfriendly to out-group believers, but rather because they are humans and humans in general are friendly to in-group members but unfriendly to out-group members. In short, the universal psychological propensity underlies both secular and religious wars.

As noted in Chapter 25, Moses orders the military officers of Israelites to kill all Midianites except virgins. The Bible reveals men's propensity to appropriate the women of another group. The propensity can be found not only in religious males but also in secular males. For example, Genghis Khan (1158-1227), the founder of the Mongol Empire, appropriated so many women from other countries that about 16 million Asians today have Genghis Khan's genes (Zerjal et al., 2003, p. 720). The propensity can also be found in some tribes in South America. According to an anthropological study on Yanomano Indians in South America (Chagnon, 1988, p. 989), warriors have 4.91 children and 1.63 wives on average, whereas nonwarriors have 1.59 children and 0.63 wives on average. Warriors have far more wives and children than nonwarriors because warriors are respected in their group and because they appropriate additional women from another group (Chagnon, 1988, p. 990).

One caveat is in order. My foregoing explanation of religious wars does not entail that it is right for a religious group to attack another religious group and for a secular group to attack another secular group. It only entails that the same psychological propensity underpins both religious and secular wars. My explanation of religious wars is compatible with the recommendation that different groups should cooperate with each other rather than attack each other.

Finally, there was a strict distinction between in-group members and out-group members in the Paleolithic Age, but there is no such distinction today due to TV, telephones, cars, airplanes, the internet, and so forth (Park, 2025, pp. 202-203). We interact with out-group members more frequently than did our Paleolithic ancestors. Moreover, out-group members can suddenly become in-group members in the modern society. Suppose, for example, that you passed a job interview in Samsung along with other applicants. You and other applicants were out-group members to each other, but you and they become in-group members to each other working in the same office. Since there is no strict line between in-group members and out-group members in the modern society, it is problematic to be unfriendly to out-group members in the way our Paleolithic ancestors were unfriendly to out-group members.

5. Summary

Wars, religious and secular, occur because we have the psychological propensity to be friendly to in-group members but unfriendly to out-group members. Those who had the psychological propensity were more likely to survive and reproduce than those who had the psychological propensity to be friendly both to in-group and out-group members in the Paleolithic Age. However, there is no strict distinction between in-group members and out-group members today, although there was the strict distinction between them in the Paleolithic Age.

Study Questions

1. Explicate the kinds of humans: parochialists and egalitarians. Who were fitter in the Paleolithic Age? How do you respond to good-natured people, such as Mother Teressa and Albert Schweitzer? Why are such people rare? Are they fitter than ordinary people?

2. Why do religious and secular wars occur? Provide a psychological answer and an evolutionary answer to this question. Do you agree or disagree with the answers? Why?

References

Chagnon, N. (1988). Life histories, blood revenge, and warfare in a tribal population. *Science*, 239(4843), 985-992.

Park, S. (2025). *Induction, science, and morality*. Cham: Springer.

Pinker, S. (2011). *Better angels of our nature: Why violence has declined*. USA: Viking Adult.

Rusch, H. (2014). The evolutionary interplay of intergroup conflict and altruism in humans: A review of parochial altruism theory and prospects for its extension. *Proceedings of the Royal Society of London B: Biological Sciences*, 281(1794), 1-9.

Zerjal, T. Xue, Y., Bertorelle, G., Wells, R., Bao, W., Zhu, S., Qamar, R., Ayub, Q., Mohyuddin, A., Fu, A., Li,P., Yuldasheva, N., Ruzibakiev, R., Xu, J., Shu, Q., Du, R., Yang, H., Hurles, M., Robinson, E., Gerelsaikhan, T., Dashnyam, B., Mehdi, S., Tyler-Smith, C. (2003). The genetic legacy of the Mongols. *The American Journal of Human Genetic*, 72(3), 717-721.

CHAPTER

28

Ego-Expanders in Religion

1. Preamble

There are ego-expanders in religion. "Ego-expander" is here defined as a statement that inclines certain individuals to feel that they are special and superior to others and to be narcissistic about themselves. The following statements are examples of religious ego-expanders:

The List of Religious Ego-Expanders

- "God created mankind in his own image" (Genesis 1:27).
- God allowed mankind to rule over "all the wild animals" (Genesis 1:26).
- God sent his son, Jesus Christ, "to save sinners" (1 Timothy 1:15).
- God has chosen "Israel to be his treasured possession" (Psalm 135:4).

The first three statements on the list are ego-expanders in that they incline humans to think that they are special and superior to nonhuman entities. However, nonhuman animals might feel indignant at it, if they could, thinking that God treats humans and nonhuman animals unfairly. The last statement on the list inclines Israelis to think that they are special and superior to non-Israelis. However, non-Israelis might feel indignant at it, thinking that God discriminates against them.

This chapter addresses the following questions about ego-expanders. Why do they exist in religion? Are there ego-expanders in secular enterprises, too? Where do religious and secular ego-expanders originate? What psychological feature accounts for their existence? Can evolutionary theory explain why we have the psychological feature? Readers will see that my answers to these questions align with cognitive science of religion, according to which the cognitive mechanism producing secular beliefs also produces religious beliefs, and the cognitive mechanism can be explained in terms of evolutionary theory.

2. Secular Ego-Expanders

In this section, I argue that ego-expanders can be found not only in religion but also in secular enterprises.

There are ego-expanders in science. For example, the Ptolemaic theory holds that the earth is at the center of the universe, and that stars and planets revolve around it. Implicit in the Ptolemaic theory is the ego-expander that God loves humans more than any other creatures, and thus humans are the most valuable beings in the cosmos.

To take a different kind of example, scientists are often dogmatic, i.e., they continue to believe that their theories are true even when they cannot explain some phenomena (Kuhn, 1962/1970, p. 144). B.F. Skinner (1904-1990) did not abandon behaviorism until he died in 1990 although it could not account for children's verbal behavior (Chomsky, 1959). Implicit in scientists' attitude is the ego-expander that they are superior to their peers.

There are ego-expanders in philosophy as well. For example, George Berkeley's (2023) idealism holds that to be is to be perceived. According to this view, a tree exists because it is perceived by humans or by God. If it were not perceived by a conscious entity, it would not exist. Implicit in idealism is the ego-expander that conscious entities, such as humans and God, are superior to nonconscious ones, such as trees and rocks.

There are ego-expanders in international politics as well. For example, the Nazis proclaimed that Germans were superior to other races. As another example, consider the name of China (中國). "Chi"(中) means center, and "na"(國) means a country or a nation. Thus, "China" means the central country. The underlying idea is that Chinese are the civilized race at the center of the world, while all the other races are barbarians. Ancient Chinese referred to Koreans, who lived to the east of China, as "Eastern Barbarians" (東夷).

There are ego-expanders in academia as well. Most professors think that their teaching ability is above average (Cross, 1977). When they receive poor scores in teaching evaluation, tend to complain that the standards for evaluation are flawed. Graduate students tend to believe that their professors are greater than other professors. Implicit in their belief is another belief that they are greater than other graduate students. Such a belief is also an ego-expander.

Human life is so saturated with ego-expanders that I am inclined to define it as a field of them. We dwell in this field for a time and then depart.

3. Explanations of Ego-Expanders

Why do we hold religious and secular ego-expanders? What is their origin? My answer is that they arise from illusory superiority. Illusory superiority is the psychological propensity to overestimate one's own qualities and abilities (Hoorens, 1993). For example, we tend to believe that we are more intelligent, more attractive, more popular, and drive better than average. Illusory superiority is responsible for both religious and secular ego-expanders.

Why do we have illusory superiority? An evolutionary explanation goes as follows. In the distant past, our ancestors did not did not have this psychological feature. At some point in time, a variation occurred, i.e., certain individuals were born with it. They fared better than those without it in the battle to survive and reproduce, i.e., it was fitness-conducive. They reproduced, passing it on to their offspring. Over time, the number of humans with it increased, while the number of humans without it decreased. As a result, it is widespread among us.

What reason is there for thinking that illusory superiority is an adaptive trait? Imagination is required to answer this question. Individuals with illusory superiority tend to think that they are superior to others, and thus that they deserve more natural resources for survival and reproduction, such as fruits and animals. In the Paleolithic Age, there were no governments to regulate their behaviors. Consequently, they invaded their neighboring groups and seized their natural resources.

The human history shows that confident individuals are more likely to persist and prosper than timid ones. For example, the English migrated to North America and subjugated the indigenous people. Russians, who lived in Europe, expanded their territory eastward all the way to Vladivostok. Spanish and Portuguese colonized Central America and South America. In the 7th century, China conquered the country called "Goguryeo" a Korean kingdom that existed in Manchuria.

Imagine that conquerors and farmers compete with each other for survival and reproduction. Conquerors believe that they are superior to others, and thus that they can rule over their neighbors. By contrast, farmers do not believe that they are superior to others, and they believe that agriculture is the foundation of all human enterprises, such as politics, art, religion, science, and business. It is clear that conquerors are fitter than farmers from an evolutionary point of view. Over time, conquerors attack neighboring farmers and then become royal and noble families, while farmers become slaves, serfs, and taxpayers.

Consider two high school students who applied for UNIST. One student possesses strong illusory superiority, while the other student possesses weak illusory superiority. In the admission interview, the former confidently tells to the interviewers that she will be a valuable asset to UNIST, and that interviewers will never regret that they have selected her over other students. By contrast, the latter does not make such a statement to interviewers. Other things being equal, the former is more likely to be accepted by UNIST than the latter.

Now imagine that there are two college students. One overestimates her abilities, while the other does not. As a result, the former aims to receive a Nobel prize in science, whereas the latter does not. The former makes some effort to achieve the aim, while the latter does not. Other things being equal, the former is more likely to receive the prize than the latter. The point of this example is that those who have high aims tend to achieve more than those who do not have such aims.

Illusory superiority also contributes to reproductive success. Imagine that there are two individuals. One believes that she is better than others as a prospective spouse, while the other does not. The former was a confident individual, while the latter, were not. The former implicitly conveys a message to her potential spouses that her future spouse will be happy with her, while the latter conveys no such message to their potential spouses. It is evident that the former is more likely to attract a mate and reproduce than the latter.

4. Objection and Reply

How would objectors respond to the evolutionary explanation that we possess illusory superiority because it was an adaptive trait? They would object that on close examination, illusory superiority is a maladaptive trait. It predisposes individuals to be arrogant. Arrogant individuals are often disliked and avoided by others. As a result, they are less likely to survive and reproduce than humble individuals.

How can this objection be refuted? We tend to be humble to acquaintances but arrogant to strangers. We regularly interact with acquaintances, but not with strangers. If we are disliked and shunned by acquaintances, our chances of survival and reproduction go down. By contrast, even if we are hated and shunned by strangers, our chances of survival and reproduction do not go down. Illusory superiority is fitness-conducive, so long as it is directed toward strangers, but not toward acquaintances.

Why is it that illusory superiority is activated when its target agents are strangers, but not activated when they are acquaintances? Future research is needed to answer this question, but a possible answer is that we have some information about our acquaintances, and thus we can judge, with some degree of accuracy, whether we are superior to them. By contrast, we lack such information about strangers, and thus we tend to assume that we are superior to them.

5. Summary

Human life is the field of ego-expanders. They exist not only in religion but also in secular enterprises. They stem from the same psychological feature, illusory superiority. We possess illusory superiority because it was fitness-conducive. Those who had it were more likely to conquer others and secure more mates than those who did not have it. It inclines individuals to be arrogant, thereby bringing down their survivability and fertility. However, it is an adaptive trait, insofar as it is activated toward strangers, but not activated toward acquaintances.

Study Questions

1. What is an ego-expander? Offer your own examples of a religious ego-expander and a secular ego-expander. What is illusory superiority? Provide your own examples to illustrate illusory superiority. What is the connection between illusory superiority and ego-expanders?

2. Offer an evolutionary explanation of why we possess illusory superiority. Provide examples for thinking that illusory superiority is an adaptive trait, and examples for thinking that it is a maladaptive

trait. Is the evolutionary explanation of illusory superiority plausible?

References

Berkeley, G. (2023). *A treatise concerning the principles of human knowledge*. Frankfurt: Megali Verlag.

Chomsky, N. (1959). Review of verbal behavior. *Language*, 35(1), 26-58.

Cross, P. (1977). Not can, but will college teaching be improved? *New Directions of Higher Education*, 19(17), 1-17.

Hoorens, V. (1993). Self-enhancement and superiority biases in social comparison. *European Review of Social Psychology*, 4(1), 113-139.

Kuhn, T. (1962/1970). *The structure of scientific revolutions*. Chicago: The University of Chicago Press.

CHAPTER

29

Religious Revolutions

1. Introduction

Religious practitioners worship morally good deities, but not morally bad ones. For example, Christians worship God, but not Satan. Why do they worship morally good deities, but not morally bad ones? This chapter answers this question from the perspective of the new field of science called "cognitive science of religion (CSR)." This chapter also answers the following related questions. Will there be religious revolutions? If so, why? If not, why not? A religious revolution is an episode in which religious practitioners stop worshiping an old deity and start worshiping a new one.

2. The Current Toolbox

In this section, I point out that the theoretical tools in the current toolbox of CSR are not sufficient to explain why religious practitioners worship morally good deities, but not morally bad ones.

CSR attempts to understand religious beliefs and behaviors in terms of the cognitive mechanisms discovered in cognitive science. The cognitive mechanisms are supposed to explain not only religious beliefs and behaviors but also secular beliefs and behaviors. A fundamental assumption of CSR is, as E. Thomas Lawson puts it, "whatever it takes to explain how minds work generally will be sufficient to explain how religious minds work" (Lawson, 2000, p. 79). Another fundamental assumption of CSR is that the cognitive mechanisms invoked to explain religious beliefs and behaviors should themselves be explained in terms of evolutionary theory.

CSR invokes multiple cognitive mechanisms to explain religious beliefs and behaviors. The most prominent ones are the hypersensitive agency detection device (Guthrie, 1993; Barrett, 2000; Atran, 2002), theory of mind (Bering, 2002), minimally counterintuitive concepts (Boyer, 1994, p. 121), and dualism (Bloom, 2005). The hypersensitive agency detection device inclines us to interpret ambiguous objects as cognitive agents. Theory of mind enables us to read our target agents' minds, i.e., to infer their mental states. Minimally counterintuitive concepts make it easier to remember supernatural entities. Dualism goes hand in hand with the religious view that there is life after bodily death.

How do I assess these theoretical resources in the current toolbox of CSR? They may be necessary and sufficient to explain why religious practitioners worship deities, but not why they worship morally good deities. As a consequence, a new cognitive mechanism is required to explain why religious practitioners worship morally good deities, but not morally bad ones.

One might put cultural influence into the toolbox, suggesting that religious practitioners worship morally good deities because their parents taught them to do so. Such an explanation, however, cries out for a further explanation. Why do their parents worship morally good deities, but not morally bad ones, and why do they teach their children to worship morally good deities, but not morally bad ones? Thus, we are back to the original question: why do religious practitioners worship morally good deities, but not morally bad ones?

One might now suggest that religious practitioners worship morally good deities, but not morally bad ones, because they have the goal to go to heaven. A problem with this explanation is that it is teleological. In a teleological explanation, a goal is invoked to explain phenomena. It is a teleological explanation, for example, that an elephant has a long nose so that it can eat grass. A teleological explanation contrasts with a mechanical explanation. In a mechanical explanation, a cause is invoked to explain phenomena. It is a mechanical explanation, for example, that an elephant has a long nose because its ancestors acquired long noses as a result of a genetic mutation. Ancient scientists, such as Aristotle, accepted both teleological and mechanical explanations. By contrast, modern scientists, such as Galileo, rejected teleological explanations and accepted mechanical explanations.

Mechanical explanations are accepted but teleological explanations are rejected in CSR, as in other contemporary scientific disciplines, such as physics and biology. In CSR, a cognitive mechanism and an evolutionary history are invoked to explain religious beliefs and actions. The cognitive mechanism and the evolutionary history are prior conditions for religious beliefs and actions, but not the goals or purposes of religious beliefs and actions. Therefore, invoking them results in mechanical explanations.

3. Why Morally Good Deities?

In this section, I postulate the existence of a new psychological mechanism to explain why religious practitioners worship morally good deities, but not morally bad ones.

As noted in Section 4 of Chapter 25, a psychological experiment on a one-year-old baby shows that the baby can tell the difference between a good guy and a bad guy, that the baby chooses a good guy over a bad guy, and that the baby even punishes a bad guy (Bloom, 2013). This experiment supports the hypothesis that we have the innate propensity to like morally good agents and to dislike bad ones, and undermines the hypothesis that we are taught to like morally good agents and to dislike bad ones.

This instinctive preference for morally good agents over morally bad ones is manifest in politics. Suppose that two presidential candidates compete with each other in a presidential election. Voters know that stakes are high, i.e., that their choice between a morally good candidate and a morally bad one will make a significant difference to their daily lives. Electing a morally good candidate as their president will bring prosperity to their country while electing a morally bad one as their president will bring adversity to their country. As a result, they instinctively choose a morally good candidate over a morally bad one.

In my view, this instinctive preference for morally good agents over morally bad ones is also operative in religion. Religious practitioners believe that their choice between morally good and morally bad deities will make a huge difference to their afterlives. For example, they believe that worshiping God will bring them eternal happiness after they die, but worshiping Satan will bring them eternal unhappiness after they die. As a result, they instinctively choose God over Satan.

This natural inclination to choose morally good agents over morally bad ones is fitness-conducive. Imagine that there were two groups of social agents in the distant past. The social agents of the first group had the natural instinct to like morally good agents and to dislike morally bad ones, so they invested their resources in morally good agents, but not in morally bad ones. By contrast, the social agents of the second group did not have the natural instinct, and they invested their resources equally in morally good and bad agents. The social agents of the first group had a better chance to survive and reproduce than those of the second group. As time passed, the descendants of the first group persisted while those of the second group perished. For this reason, we have the innate propensity to like morally good agents and to dislike morally bad ones, and religious practitioners today worship morally good deities, but not morally bad ones.

4. Religious Revolutions will Occur

In this section, I present the scriptural evidence to show that the deities that current religious practitioners worship are not morally perfect, and then present the reason for predicting that future religious practitioners will stop worshiping old deities and start worshiping new ones who are morally better than old ones.

There are many hateful verses in the Bible and in the Quran. The Bible states, to cite a few, that heretics "must be destroyed" (Exodus 22:20), non-virgin brides should be stoned "to death" (Deuteronomy 22:21), and that witches should not be allowed "to live" (Exodus 22:18). The same holds for Allah. The Quran states, to cite a few, that you should "kill the polytheists wherever you find them" (9:5), and that "Allah has cursed the disbelievers and prepared for them a Blaze" (33: 64). Such verses in the Bible and in the Quran indicate that God and Allah are not morally perfect, and motivate us to predict that there will be religious revolutions, i.e., future religious practitioners will worship new deities in the future, say, millions of years from now.

Suppose that genetic mutations will occur to our descendants. As a result, some babies will be born with a higher standard of morality than other babies, and they will impose it on their target agents. As a result, the target agents that they will like will be morally better than the target agents that their competitors will like. Under such conditions, they will have a better chance to survive and reproduce than their competitors. Their psychological propensity will be passed on to next generations. If enough time passes, their descendants will persist while their competitors' descendants will perish, and there will only be humans who will impose the higher standard of morality on their target agents

As a consequence, future religious practitioners will resist old deities, such as God and Allah, thinking that old deities are not morally good enough to deserve their worship. They will conceive of new deities who will be morally better than old ones. After conceiving of new deities, they will worship them. In short, religious revolutions will occur. Religious revolutions will be due to the two factors. First, old deities will fail to meet a higher standard of morality that future religious practitioners will impose on target agents. Second, future religious practitioners will conceive of new deities who will meet the higher standard of morality and who will be morally better than old ones.

It is not difficult to imagine new deities who are morally better than God and Allah. Deities who oppose killing heretics are morally better than God and Allah, other things being equal. Consider also that God allegedly sends believers to heaven and disbelievers to hell. In my view, it is unfair for him to issue only the two extreme grades – eternal happiness and unhappiness – to his evaluatees. A just deity would recognize that his evaluatees deserve reward and punishment to different degrees. As a result, he would create numerous places which are similar to heaven and hell to different degrees, and then would send his evaluatees to appropriate places depending on how much they deserve happiness and unhappiness. This evaluation system is far more fine-grained, and hence more just, than God's evaluation system.

How probable is it that religious revolutions will occur? A scientific study of genes and future environments is required to estimate the probability of religious revolutions. We would have to know what genes are responsible for the innate propensity to like morally good agents and to dislike morally bad ones, what mechanisms underlie genetic mutations, and what the future environment will be like. Due to the lack of such knowledge, we cannot gauge the probability that the aforementioned genetic mutations will occur and hence the probability that religious revolutions will occur.

However, it is more than a mere speculation that religious revolutions will occur. Our standard of morality has been getting higher and higher, and thus we can reasonably predict that our standard of morality will continue to get higher and higher. As Steven Pinker notes, 15% of human beings were murdered before the emergence of states, but only 3% of human beings were murdered in the 20th century (Pinker, 2011, pp. 48-50). There were many horrible practices in the past, such as sacrificing human beings to deities, witch-hunting, and burying human beings alive with dead kings. They no longer exist in the present. Consequently, it is reasonable to predict that religious practitioners will reach a point at which they will take it seriously that their old deities do not meet their standard of morality.

5. No Religious Revolution will Occur

In this section, I postulate the existence of another new psychological mechanism to explain why current religious practitioners worship their deities despite the scriptural evidence that their deities are not morally perfect, and then present the reason for predicting that no religious revolution will occur in the future.

We praise or blame moral agents around us depending on whether they are morally good or bad. We praise them, for example, for paying taxes and blame them for evading taxes. However, we praise and blame them to different degrees depending on how powerful they are. We criticize the weak, e.g., restaurant owners, freely and harshly for evading taxes, not fearing that they might retaliate against us. By contrast, we do not criticize the strong, e.g., prosecutors, as freely and harshly as we criticize the weak, fearing that they might retaliate against us with their power. In short, we have the innate propensity to be respectful to the strong and to be disrespectful to the weak.

The innate propensity is also operative in the international community. Suppose that a weak country invades another weak country, killing one million innocent civilians. We freely and severely criticize the invading country, not fearing that the invading country might retaliate against us. Suppose now that a strong country invades another country, killing one million innocent civilians. We do not criticize the strong country as freely and severely as we criticize the weak country, fearing that the invading country might retaliate against us.

The innate propensity can also be found in religion. Religious practitioners do not criticize their deities despite the scriptural evidence that their deities are not morally perfect. Such phenomena are not surprising, given that they believe that their deities are omnipotent, and given that the degree of our criticism to our target agents is inversely proportional to the degree of the power of our target agents. Religious practitioners even have a special term "blasphemy" for discouraging people from criticizing their deities.

How do religious practitioners respond to hateful verses in scriptures? One popular response is to ignore them and to stick to the belief that their deities are morally perfect. This popular response to hateful verses in scriptures is an indication that they are lenient with their deities, and that they are respectful to the strong.

Another popular response is to argue that hateful verses in scriptures should be interpreted metaphorically, and thus that the afore-cited hateful verses from the Bible and the Quran do not mean that religious practitioners should kill heretics. They just mean that religious practitioners do not need to treat heretics in the way they treat religious in-group members, or something like that.

This popular response is problematic. There are other verses in scriptures that religious practitioners would want to interpret literally. For example, the Bible states, "God created the heavens and the earth" (Genesis 1:1). They would not interpret this sentence metaphorically and say that God did not create the world. They would rather interpret it literally and say that he created the world. Therefore, they should come up with a criterion for distinguishing between the verses that we should interpret metaphorically and the verses that we should interpret literally. Otherwise, it is arbitrary to interpret hateful verses metaphorically and other verses literally.

However, it is a difficult task to come up with the criterion. In consequence, it is reasonable to predict that religious practitioners will interpret hateful verses metaphorically and other verses literally without presenting the criterion. From their perspective, taking the arbitrary position is better than taking the unsavory position that their deities are not morally perfect. This popular response to hateful verses in scriptures indicates that they are dogmatic.

Why do we have the innate propensity to be respectful to the strong and to be disrespectful to the weak? An evolutionary answer goes as follows. Our distant ancestors acquired the innate propensity as a result of a variation. They were fitter than their rivals. The innate propensity was passed on to next generations. After many generations, those who had the innate propensity persisted while those who did not perished. For this reason, we have the innate propensity.

6. Summary

Religious practitioners worship morally good deities, but not morally bad ones, because humans have the innate propensity to like morally good agents and to dislike morally bad ones. Religious practitioners today worship their deities, despite the scriptural evidence that they are not morally perfect, because humans have the innate propensity to be respectful to the strong and to be disrespectful to the weak. Both propensities are fitness-conducive.

It is not clear whether religious revolutions will occur. If the first propensity defeats the second one, religious revolutions will occur, and future religious practitioners will worship new deities who will be morally better than old ones. By contrast, if the balance is kept between the two propensities or if the second propensity becomes stronger than the first propensity, no religious revolution will occur, and future religious practitioners will worship old deities that current religious practitioners worship. In any event, the hypotheses about the two psychological propensities should be put into the toolbox of CSR.

Study Questions

1. Give the psychological and evolutionary explanations of why religious practitioners worship morally good deities, but not bad ones. Are the explanations agreeable or disagreeable to you?

Why?

2. How do you respond to the prediction that our distant descendants will worship new deities who will be morally better than old one, and to the prediction that they will not? Do you have an alternative prediction?

References

Atran, S. (2002). *In gods we trust: The evolutionary landscape of religion*. Oxford: Oxford University Press.

Barrett, J. (2004). *Why would anyone believe in God?* Walnut Creek, CA: AltaMira Press.

Bering J. (2002). The existential theory of mind. *Review of General Psychology*, 6(1), 3-24.

Bloom, P. (2013). *Just babies: The origins of good and evil*. New York: Broadway Books.

Boyer, P. (1994). *The naturalness of religious ideas*. Berkeley: University of California Press.

Guthrie, S. (1993). *Faces in the clouds*. New York: Oxford University Press.

Kuhn, T. (1962/1970). *The structure of scientific revolutions*. Chicago: University of Chicago Press.

Lawson, E. T. (2000). Cognition. In W. Braun and R. McCutcheon (Eds.), *Guide to the study of religion* (pp. 75-84). London: Cassell.

Pinker, S. (2011). *Better angels of our nature: Why violence has declined*. USA: Viking Adult.

30

CHAPTER

Is Philosophy of Religion Useful to Religion?

1. Questions

Philosophy of religion is an attempt to understand religion from a philosophical perspective, examining the fundamental assumptions of religion, such as the assumption that God created the world and the assumption that he sends believers and disbelievers to heaven and to hell, respectively. Is philosophy of religion useful or useless to religion? Does philosophy of religion have to be useful or useless to religion? This chapter aims to answer these questions.

2. Opposing Views

Believers would claim that philosophy of religion is useless to religion. Philosophers of religion criticize fundamental religious beliefs, such as the belief that God created the universe and the belief that believers go to heaven and disbelievers go to hell. Philosophy of religion is destructive of religion. Hence, it is useless to religion.

Contrary to this expectation, Alvin Plantinga (1932-present), a Christian and renowned philosopher of religion, claims that philosophy of religion is useful to religion. In his view, philosophy of religion provides believers with the opportunity to think about how their religious beliefs are related to nonreligious belief, e.g., scientific beliefs. In addition, philosophy of religion provides believers with the theoretical resources to defend religious beliefs. For example, the problem of other minds in philosophy mind holds that we do not have sufficient evidence for the belief that other people have minds. Utilizing this problem, Plantinga (1990) argues that just as we can justifiably believe that other people have minds, so we can justifiably believe that God exists (Chapter 10).

3. Different Enterprises

How do I respond to the debate over whether philosophy of religion is useful or useless to religion? I construct the following argument. Religion has its own aims and methods. So does philosophy of religion. Therefore, religion and philosophy of religion are independent enterprises, which implies that one might be valuable, even if it is useless to the other, and vice versa. Let me flesh out this argument in this section.

Religion aims to provide people with spiritual comfort and to spread religious beliefs to the world. Religion uses diverse methods to achieve these aims. For example, believers blindly trust a scripture. They are dogmatic, i.e., they do not question their core religious beliefs, such as the belief that God exists. They perform religious rituals together to foster religious beliefs and to cement social relations between them.

By contrast, philosophy of religion aims to determine whether fundamental religious beliefs are true or false, and aims to cast light on why religious people behave as they do. Philosophy of religion uses the methods of debate and discussion to achieve these aims.

Any idea is open to criticism. There is no such thing as a scripture. Blind belief is to be avoided. In short, philosophy of religion provides a space for foundational inquiries into religion.

As a consequence, there is an important difference between religious leaders, such as ministers and nuns, and philosophers of religion. Religious leaders are interested in whether other people believe in God, and they aim to persuade them into believing in him. By contrast, philosophers of religion are interested in helping them improve their intellectual power and in see what they did not see before.

The relationship between religion and philosophy of religion can be compared to the relationship between religion and literature (novels, poems, etc.). Religion and literature are independent enterprises. Religion has its own aims and methods. So does literature. It follows that even if one is useless to the other, it might be valuable, and vice versa. The same holds for religion and philosophy of religion.

Philosophy of religion may be useful to some people, whether they are believers or nonbelievers. Or it may be useless to other people, whether they are believers or nonbelievers. The bottom line is that it is not meant to be useful to religion, nor is it meant to be useless to religion. The impact of philosophy of religion on religion, whether positive or negative, is merely its by-product.

The same is true of literature. Literature may be useful to some people, whether they are believers or nonbelievers. Or it may be useless to other people, whether they are believers or nonbelievers. It is not meant to be useful to religion, nor is it meant to be useless to religion. The impact of literature on religion, whether positive or negative, is merely its by-product.

Similar stories can be given of science and philosophy of science. Some scientists claim that philosophy of science is useful to science, while other scientists claim that philosophy of science is useless to science. My response to scientists' opposing views about philosophy of science is to say that philosophy of science is neither meant to be useful nor meant to be useless to science any more than sports, dance, art, and music are meant to be useful or useless to science (Park, 2022, p. 207).

4. The Evolutionary Justification vs. the Theistic Justification

Science and religion are different enterprises with different aims and methods. In addition, science is not intended to be useful to religion any more than religion is intended to be useful to science. However, let me finish this book with an example in which science helps religion.

It is well-known in evolutionary biology that diversity is conducive to fitness. Imagine that there are two groups of human beings: Group 1 and Group 2. All the members of Group 1 are uniform in terms of their physical constitutions. All the members of Group 2 are diverse in terms of their physical constitutions.

A particular kind of germs attacks both groups. All the members of Group 1 are vulnerable to the germs. As a result, all of them die. By contrast, some members of Group 2 are immune to the germs, while other members of Group 2 are susceptible to them. As a result, the former live while the latter die. In a nutshell, all the members of Group 1 perish, while some members of Group 2 persist.

This imaginary example illustrates that a group of diverse members has a better chance to persist than a group of uniform members, i.e., that diversity increases the probability that a group of organisms persists. The more diverse members a group has, the more likely it is that the group will persist.

This thesis can be applied to religion. Imagine that there are three groups of human beings: Group 1, Group 2, and Group 3. Group 1 consists of both theists and atheists. Group 2 only consists of theists. Group 3 only consists of atheists. We do not know how the environment will change in the future, but we can reasonably predict that Group 1 will be more likely to persist than Group 2 and Group 3. Consequently, theists and atheists are justified in adhering to theism and atheism, respectively.

This evolutionary argument for belief in God is similar to Pascal's argument for belief in him. Recall that according to Pascal's Wager, we should believe in him, although we do not have good evidence for belief in him, because we might be evaluated by him after we die. Pascal's argument for belief in him and my evolutionary argument for belief in him are summarized as follows.

<u>**Pascal's Theistic Argument**</u>

God might reward believers and punish disbelievers.

∴ We should believe in him.

<u>**My Evolutionary Argument**</u>

Diversity increases the chance that the human species will persist.

∴ Some of us should believe in God.

Pascal and I agree that we do not have good evidence for belief in God, and that belief in him might be useful. On Pascal's account, it might be useful in that it might be a ticket to heaven. On my account, it might be useful in that it might be a ticket for the persistence of the human species in the future environment.

There are two noteworthy differences between Pascal's theistic argument and my evolutionary argument. First, Pascal's argument claims that all of us should believe in God, while my evolutionary argument claims that some of us should believe in him. Second, Pascal's theistic argument appeals to the speculative assumption that he might reward believers and punish disbelievers after they die, while my evolutionary argument appeals to the scientific theory, evolutionary theory.. However, it is also a speculative assumption that belief in him might be helpful to believers in the future environment.

5. Summary

Philosophers of religion defend and attack the fundamental religious beliefs. In this sense, philosophy of religion is both useful and useless to religion. However, religion and philosophy of religion are independent enterprises in the sense that they have different aims and use different methods to achieve those aims. Philosophy of religion is neither meant to be useful to religion nor meant to be useless to religion any more than literature is meant to be useful or useless to religion.

There is an example in which a scientific idea helps religion. A group whose members are diverse has a better chance to persist than another group whose members are uniform. Consequently, the human species has a better chance to persist when there are theists and atheists than when there are only theists or only atheists. This argument for belief in God appeals to a scientific theory while Pascal's argument for belief in him appeals to a speculative assumption that he might evaluate us after we die.

Study Questions

1. What are the aims of religion and the aims of philosophy of religion?

What methods do religion and philosophy of religion use to achieve those aims? Does philosophy of religion have to be useful to religion?

2. What are the similarities and differences between the theistic argument for belief in God and the evolutionary argument for belief in him? Which is more convincing to you? Why? You are welcome to criticize one of them or both.

References

Park, S. (2022). *Embracing scientific realism*. Cham: Springer.

Plantinga, A. (1990). *God and other minds: A study of the rational justification of belief in God*. Ithaca: Cornell University Press.

About the Author

Homepage: https://philpeople.org/profiles/seungbae-park

Seungbae Park is a philosophy professor at Ulsan National Institute of Science and Technology in the Republic of Korea. He received his Ph.D. from the University of Arizona in 2001, specializing in philosophy of science under the guidance of Professor Richard Healey. He taught at the University of Arizona, the University of Maryland, and POSTECH, before coming to his current institution in 2009.

He published about 80 papers in SCI-level international journals. Most of them are in philosophy of science, and some of them are in philosophy of religion and ethics. He also published a book titled *Embracing Scientific Realism* in Spring in 2022 and *Induction, Science, and Morality* in Springer in 2025.

As an anonymous referee, he reviewed book manuscripts for Springer, Routledge, and Cambridge University Press, and reviewed article manuscripts for *Journal of Philosophy*, *Philosophy of Science*, *The British Journal for the Philosophy of Science*, *Synthese*, *Social Epistemology*, and *Journal of Ethics*.

Reflections upon Religion

초판인쇄 2026년 1월 2일
초판발행 2026년 1월 2일

지 은 이 Seungbae Park
펴 낸 이 채종준
펴 낸 곳 한국학술정보(주)
주 소 경기도 파주시 회동길 230(문발동)
전 화 031-908-3181(대표)
팩 스 031-908-3189
투고문의 ksibook1@kstudy.com
등 록 제일산-115호(2000. 6. 19)

ISBN 979-11-7457-308-7 93160

책에 대한 더 나은 생각, 끊임없는 고민, 독자를 생각하는 마음으로 보다 좋은 책을 만들어갑니다.